Bizarre
CARS

Bizarre
CARS

THE STRANGEST VEHICLES OF ALL TIME

KEITH RAY

The
History
Press

This book is dedicated to my wife, Teresa, and son, Marcus, who throughout have provided understanding and support to an incurable 'petrol head'.

First published 2013

The History Press
The Mill, Brimscombe Port
Stroud, Gloucestershire, GL5 2QG
www.thehistorypress.co.uk

British Library Cataloguing in Publication Data.
A catalogue record for this book is available from the British Library.

ISBN 978 0 7524 8771 7

Typesetting and origination by The History Press
Printed in China

IMPORTANT NOTICE!

The publisher wishes to point out that no car designers were harmed in the research and writing of this book. Upon reading the book, however, readers may decide that perhaps some should have been!

Foreword
by Tim Brooke-Taylor

This foreword isn't going to start well. In fact, it's going to start very badly indeed. I'M NOT PARTICULARLY INTERESTED IN CARS.

There, I've said it. But, having now read Keith's book, I realise I'd never been aware of interesting cars, I just knew very ordinary, boringly sensible, mass-production cars. I now know I was missing a lot. Take 'the Beast' for example. I love this contraption, not just because it has a 27-litre Rolls-Royce Merlin aero engine, but because it ends up looking like Del Boy's van stretched to the length of a football pitch (see page 44). It seems to have four wheels, though. I want one.

I also want a Rumpler Tropfenwagen. I want it just so I can say, in a casual throwaway manner, 'I drive a Rumpler Tropfenwagen, what do you drive? Oh, a Mondeo. How fascinating.' And who could possibly turn down some genuinely named Japanese beauties (I believe Keith when he says they're genuine, but only just). How about, for example, going for a spin in my new Mitsubishi Chariot Grandio Super Exceed? Or maybe you'd prefer to step into a Mazda Bongo Brawny and Friedee? No, I think I'd prefer to cross America

in a Daihatsu Charade Social Pose or even a Toyota Deliboy (is this another offshoot of the Trotter family or a young lad from India?).

I wonder what sort of person was on the Nissan 'naming committee' and what sort of names were on their shortlist – Harold and Maude, Crabtree and Evelyn, Brooke and Taylor, perhaps – that led them to Cedric and Gloria! What was their thinking? What name would appeal to the English-speaking countries? Something from P.G. Wodehouse maybe? A duke, Cedric, and his flighty actress friend Gloria? Perfect. It's hard to believe, though, that these names stuck for forty-four years.

Imagine yourself, as I did a couple of days ago, driving down the M3 and suddenly being overtaken by the Aerocar N101D, the Fairthorpe Atom and the Bond Bug. It would seem like an alien attack from outer space.

Thank you, Keith, you have introduced me to a whole new universe, and my world is definitely a much better place.

Introduction

This book is about vehicles which are bizarre. That is, cars which are eccentric, fantastic, grotesque, or simply inappropriate or irrelevant – or in some cases all of the above. It is about vehicles which were simply not 'fit for purpose' for one reason or another. Many lists have been compiled of strange or bizarre cars, but all have been about cars *intended* to be bizarre or weird, such as cars which look like potting sheds, double beds, Coke bottles or oranges. This book is different. All the vehicles featured here were intended to be serious propositions, hard though it may be to believe. This did not, however, prevent them from entering the world of the truly bizarre.

Now, I am not saying these vehicles were bad as such. Conversely, some of them, in their own way, were very good indeed. An excellent example is the Scammell Contractor Bus/Truck. It worked fine as a vehicle, carrying workers and goods for South African State Railways. But it was arguably the finest super-heavy haulage tractor of its day, an enormous great lump of metal with a hideously powerful engine that could potentially haul medium-sized European countries across continents, up gradients steeper than the side of the Empire State Building, while doing little more than idling over. So why, in heaven's name, turn it into a mundane omnibus?

Another fine vehicle was the Lancia Thema 8.32. It was incredibly fast with superb handling, but in terms of price it was in a totally different galaxy from normal car-buying folk. If you are going to spend half the National Debt on a car with a highly strung prima donna of a 3.2-litre V8 Ferrari engine under the bonnet, wouldn't you want your neighbours to know what it is and how much you spent on it? But the marketing people at Lancia decided, in their wisdom, to make it look identical to the bog-standard Thema. The only distinguishing feature was a little badge on the boot, about the size of a second-class postage stamp, which declared '8.32'. It was a bit like putting a Rolex movement inside a gaudy plastic Swatch case. I suspect the 8 in the 8.32 is the number of cars they sold in the UK, and the 32 is the average IQ of the purchasers.

At the other end of the spectrum, the Russians have produced some real gems. One of my personal favourites is the ZIS 101 Sport. This was an open two-seater version of the ZIS limousine built for the top Soviet officials. The limousine was over 20ft long and weighed around 4 tons, and it was definitely 'fit for purpose'. But when they produced the two-seat version, it did not occur to the marketing geniuses to make it just a tad shorter and lighter. Hence the longest and heaviest two-seater sports car of all time.

Also from ZIS and ZIL (as ZIS became known once the Soviets realised Stalin, for whom the 'S' stood, wasn't Mother Teresa after all) came another of my favourites, the ZIL sports racing car. When they came to this model they did make it shorter than the limousine, but preserved all the styling excesses of enormous fins and monumental radiator grille. However, shortened limousines don't make good racing cars, and up against things like the E-type Jaguars and Ferraris of the time, it was an unmitigated disaster. It was rumoured that the Ministry of Defence was considering replacing the nuclear missile programme with a fleet of ZIS 101 Sports. They believed that parking these vehicles near the front line in any conflict would render the Cold War enemy so completely helpless with laughter that military opposition would prove impossible.

There is one point I must stress again at the outset. Many people have built cars to be deliberately bizarre, like Edd China with his superb double bed and garden shed on wheels, and advertising vehicles which look like hamburgers or oranges. But they were all meant to be silly. Every car in this book was genuinely intended to be a serious offering to the motoring public.

Some of the most bizarre cars are not very well known today, and this book should help preserve their memory as a cautionary tale for car designers. Some are better known and a few are, bizarrely, still in production. Bizarreness on wheels is not confined to certain countries or certain eras. It appears to have touched most sectors of the motoring market worldwide at some time.

So, let's now delve into the archives of the truly bizarre.

A Typology of Automotive Bizarreness

This book has been arranged around a typology of bizarreness. It was not an easy task, as nearly all the vehicles covered here could easily have been placed in the final category: plain bonkers. But after careful thought, and a fine bottle or two of Chateau Petrolhead Twin Cam 1998, the following categories emerged:

Bizarski: The Eastern Block
Russia and the other former Communist Eastern European countries have produced some of the most bizarre vehicles ever, possibly because 'consumer choice', as we now understand the term, simply did not exist … well, it did exist, but most of those expressing a 'consumer choice' ended up pursuing a highly successful career in salt mining.

What Sell-By Date?
Some vehicles are truly bizarre because the designers and manufacturers completely lost all sense of time, on a scale akin to Noah coming back today to run an animal sanctuary in Torquay.

Simple Overkill

A number of vehicles have been included here because of what might be called 'simple overkill'. Exactly what this means will become evident. Think along the lines of an electric toothbrush being converted to run from a 250hp V8 outboard motor, for example, and you'll get my point.

Bizarreness on an Imperial Chinese Scale

Despite being the world's most populous country, and now having the world's largest car market, China only has six representatives here, and one is not even a car. However, the lack of numerical representation is more than compensated for by the degree of bizarreness involved.

Misunderstanding the Market

This is actually the largest category, even larger than the 'plain bonkers' one. It is as if there's a whole load of car designers who never leave their bedrooms, keep the curtains tightly drawn, have no friends, live on their computers and indeed have little understanding of what the word 'people' actually means.

Two-Wheeled Bizarreness

Motorcycles and other two-wheeled vehicles don't get off scot free here. There have been some truly bizarre examples with just two wheels.

Bizarreness at the Cutting-Edge

This is in many ways the specialist VIP category, populated by vehicles whose bizarreness really pushes back the boundaries of normality, right into the sphere of bizarre nirvana.

Bizarreness in Very Small Helpings

Before Alec Issigonis shocked the motoring world by demonstrating that a small car can actually look like, and be like, a normal car rather than a converted wheelbarrow or dodgem car, the small car sector of the market was full of truly bizarre offerings ... including, for example, cars which were converted wheelbarrows and dodgem cars.

Plain Bonkers

Finally, the 'catch-all' category for vehicles which don't obviously fit into any of the other categories, but which were just plain, simple, unadulterated bonkers!

Bizarski: The Eastern Block

I'll begin with one of my favourites, the ZIS 101 Sport. From Stalin's day up until the collapse of the Soviet Union in 1991, the Soviet leaders had a need for hideously large hyper-mega-barges to whisk them from one member state to another in order to suppress the odd local uprising, banish the occasional million to the salt mines in Siberia, and show the downtrodden peasants that the Politburo members were the absolute dog's bollockski. They had the perfect solution, the ZIS 101. About 20ft long and weighing 3.5 tons, it was nearly large enough to accommodate a full performance of the Bolshoi Ballet. It was absolutely 'fit for purpose'. It was the car Stalin used as his personal transport. Any vague similarity to the absolutely identical Packard Super 8 was dismissed as pure coincidence by the guys at ZIS.

The rare cabriolet version of the ZIS 101 Sport. (Courtesy of Adam Kliczek)

I have always rather liked the series of enormous limos the Russians produced for their leaders. They have a raw, brutal strength about them and look as though they were chiselled slowly from a solid block of Ukrainian steel by muscular young women in dungarees, which they probably were.

Now, one day the marketing guys at ZIS (did they have marketing departments in a state where there was no choice?) thought it would be a sound business idea to extend the product range beyond presidential mega-barges, so what did they choose? An oil tanker on wheels? A 200-corpse mega-hearse? A mobile oil-drilling platform? No, they thought it would be an absolutely corking idea to do an open two-seater sports version, the ZIS 101 Sport.

It seems the only man with access to the hacksaw at the ZIS factory was off sick that day, so rather than produce a short-wheelbase chassis, they were stuck with the 3.5-ton, 20ft+ behemoth. Then the designers got to work. In order to make the sports car look a little less like a shoe driving in reverse, they decided to place the two seats in the middle by inserting an extension between the bonnet and the scuttle large enough for a Soyuz V spacecraft launch pad. Then they had to fill the space between the two seats and the rear, a space so long you might walk between two different time zones to put your luggage in the boot.

You can see that the front and rear wings, and the running board between, are exactly as on the limo. It is the longest two-seat car in history. The fact that it looked like an impossibly long phallic symbol, did about 100yd to the gallon and cost as much to buy as a medium-sized Eastern European country did limit the market potential just a tad. One intrepid owner is reputed to have driven from Minsk to Moscow, only to find Red Square was too narrow for him to do a three-point turn. I don't know if any survive.

It will be some time before we see an open two-seat 'sports' barge to match the ZIS 101 Sport, if ever. It's certainly 'one up' on your typical, boring Porsche 911 or Jaguar XK. It is a real credit to that army of muscular young Soviet ladies in dungarees with their cold chisels and hammers.

The Car That Could Only Turn Right

In 1912 the Russian Count Pyotr Schilovski visited the Wolseley factory in England with the design for a two-wheeled gyroscopically stabilised car. The Wolseley guys were clearly impressed and embarked immediately on building a prototype. It was powered by a modified Wolseley C5 engine of 16–20hp. Unfortunately, few contemporary photographs survive.

The Gyrocar deserves inclusion as a bizarre car on a number of counts:

1   The Count claimed it would be of great military value as it could cross terrain that four-wheeled vehicles couldn't. However, as it weighed 2.75 tons, and all this weight was concentrated on just two bicycle-sized wheels, the claim seems dubious. 'Sink without trace' might be more appropriate than 'great military value'. Maybe the Count didn't know what the word 'terrain' meant.

2   The gyroscope flywheel weighed 12cwt and was 40in in diameter. Its great weight meant that 10% of the engine's modest power output was absorbed in simply rotating the flywheel.

3   Although it had a transmission brake, there were no other conventional brakes on the wheels to stop its 2.75 tons.

4   Its turning circle was about the size of Yorkshire.

5   The most bizarre feature was arguably a technical aspect of gyroscopes, whereby movements in one direction can cause forces in a direction at right angles; it's called precession. Complicated to understand, but the practical implication of this was that the Gyrocar was unable to turn left. Turning right was a doddle, but turning left would make the whole thing

flip up in the air, depositing the unfortunate gyronauts on the road. Now I know, in theory, you can go from any 'A' to any 'B' (eventually) by just turning right all the time, but I suspect this would not have endeared the Gyrocar to the general public.

6 It must be one of the few cars ever made which had stabilisers like a kiddy's bike. These were in case the driver left the vehicle with its engine running but without turning off the gyros. In these circumstances the Gyrocar would balance for a while, and then topple over, which could be most unfortunate for any remaining occupants.

7 Finally, it must have felt distinctively uncomfortable for the driver having a 12cwt, brittle cast-iron flywheel rotating at 2,000rpm just beneath his private parts.

After just two years, at the outbreak of the First World War, it was put into storage by being buried – not a recommended storage technique for any car. A long time after the war, in 1938, they went to dig it up only to find someone had built a railway on top of it; again, not too good for the bodywork. It was eventually retrieved and restored, and was displayed at Wolseley's company museum. Sadly, it was broken up in 1948, never to be seen again.

Had the Gyrocar idea caught on, I imagine today we'd see 40-ton gyrotrucks and 100-seat plus gyro double-decker buses tearing down the M1, precariously balanced on just a couple of slim wheels. Not a very comfortable prospect.

The old Soviet bloc was quite good at building ancient tractor-like cars with all the comfort of a Siberian Gulag and the style of a plastic toilet brush. But they worked, and they kept going and going. OK, the engine was designed a few decades before Noah commissioned his Ark and they handled like a wet bar of soap in a hot shower. But they were at least 'honest'. You knew what you were getting – which was unadulterated crap.

Take the Pobeda 20, made from 1945 (by which time it was already a historic relic in danger of entering the fossil record) up until 1958. It was a frumpy, 2.1-litre, 4-cylinder Soviet barge weighing in at nearly 1.5 tons, so its 50bhp took some persuading to get the beast out of the stationary position. It would get to around 59mph if you had a couple of days to spare, but at that speed you took your life into your own hands if words like 'corner', 'brake' or 'stop' ever came to mind.

OK, it looked shit, and it was. But the marketing guys at Pobeda weren't happy about that. They wanted something sexier; a GAZ with attitude and charisma. So they introduced the Pobeda GAZ 20 Sport, a racy two-door with real sex appeal (see right). Maybe they'd been chatting to the guys at ZIS.

They took the basic Pobeda GAZ 20 (you can see the bonnet line hasn't changed at all) and covered it with 100m of cheap cooking foil. It still had the same agricultural engine, and still took two or three days to reach 59mph. But now you couldn't take corners even if you were brave enough lest the wings and tail fell off. In any case, those front wheel spats limited the steering movement to about 2 degrees left or right, so the turning circle was around 5.5 miles. Inside it was marginally less appealing than a rundown geriatric home, and one with virtually no windows. It is amazing how the designers could have taken such a bad car and been so extraordinarily successful at making it worse. I think it was called 'Sport' because you'd have to be quite a sport to try driving it. Luckily, this prototype never made it into production.

Pobeda GAZ 20. The world's least exciting car? (Courtesy of Tomas Cekanavicius)

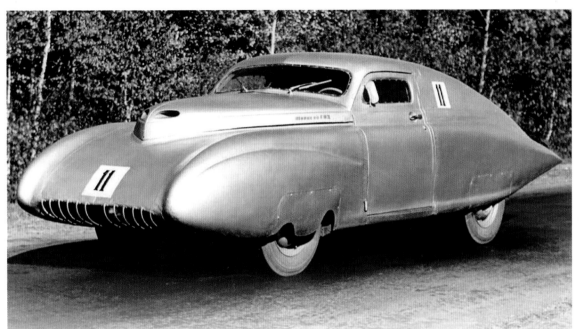

Bizarrely, the Poles took a liking to the original GAZ 20 and continued to make it, under licence under the Warszawa brand name, up until 1964, by which time it must have looked about as up to date as the Dead Sea Scrolls in PC World. Maybe it reflects what 'choice' meant in 1960s Poland. I bet they really wanted the Sport version instead. I could see it as a potential Le Mans 24-hour entrant … well, in the sense that it would have taken 24 hours to complete the first lap, provided all the cooking foil remained in place.

Can't Afford A Bentley Continental GT or Range Rover?

The Pobeda Gaz 20 was absolute crap, but it was at least honest crap. The fair imitation of the Bentley Continental GT, shown below, is actually a rebuilt Pobeda GAZ 20.

However, if you are so poor you cannot even stretch to a Range Rover, never mind a Bentley, the

GAZ 20 comes to the rescue again. OK, maybe it lacks a few of the finer points of the Range Rover, like everything except four wheels, but armed with a set of wheels like that, who's going to argue the finer points?

The Soviet E-Type Eater

In the early 1960s the ZIL factory decided to enter the field of sports car racing. The first car we commemorated in this book was the ZIS 101 Sport, maybe the most ludicrous two-seat sports car ever to have 'graced' the world's roads. Building on this epic achievement, the design guys decided to base their new challenger in the world of E-type Jaguars and Ferrari GTOs on the ZIL 111, the splendid vehicle shown here in convertible form.

The new sports car was thankfully reduced in length, and a little in weight, although I believe it still

weighed over 2.5 tons. But the tail fins remain – see how unchanged they are from the limo-barge? And its brakes were about as effective as damp digestive biscuits. Apparently it was so buttock-clenchingly awful and embarrassing that the guys at ZIL decided to axe it immediately and destroy the evidence.

Now, most readers are going to say 'What the **** is that? The Sachsen-something-or-other P240?' It's an understandable reaction, so I will provide a little background explanation.

The Sachsenring was manufactured by VEB Kraftfahrzeugwerk Horch Zwickau, based in East Germany, which brought into the world one of its best-known and most recognisable cars, the Trabant. OK, so the Trabant was made of second-hand Formica kitchen worktops, cardboard and kids' play dough, but over 4 million were made, and any East German willing to sacrifice twenty years of salary, pawn his grandmother and never eat again could afford the down payment to buy one. It was such a mind-blowingly, unremittingly awful car it was hard to dislike it. It had real personality. And you can still see some belching around the roads of Germany today.

So to the P240. Alongside the Trabant, Sachsenring decided to produce a second model. So what did they choose to be the brother of the Bakelite Tonka toy in an economy so weak it took the average factory worker five years to earn his bus fare home each evening? Yes, you guessed it – a large, luxury saloon: the P240.

It looked like a Trabant on steroids. It had a 6-cylinder, four-stroke, 2,407cc engine sourced from Horch, delivering a dazzlingly conservative 80bhp, or 33bhp per litre. It came as a saloon, estate or cabriolet. To boost sales they tried to call it the Horch Trabant Sachsenring P240. It didn't work, partly because the youngest person who could remember the once-celebrated brand name Horch was already about 98 years old. It didn't sell very well. I wonder why?

The Soviet Union: A Bizarre Car Market

Prior to the fall of the Soviet Union, the car market in the USSR certainly had a few bizarre features about it. Firstly, the names of the car companies. For some inexplicable reason – which I'm tempted to put down to the fact that in the Soviet days no car worker was sober for more than about 10 minutes at a stretch – nearly all the companies had names which were three initials: GAZ, VAZ, ZIL, ZIM, ZIS, LAZ, PAZ, RAF, MAZ, YaG, KIM, UAZ, ZAZ and BAZ, to name quite a few.

The second feature, which probably explains the lack of worker morale, was that you couldn't simply choose a car and buy it. There was a strict hierarchy: the ZIL was for the top officials, able to use the 'ZIL lanes'; the GAZ Chaika was for senior officials; then there was the Volga, Moskvitch and Lada, right down to the humble ZAZ Zaporozhets, which were about one step up from a motorised lawnmower. You bought what you were allowed to buy, except that nobody could even afford that.

To that extent it wasn't a car 'market' at all; a market is where a range of things are on offer, and you can buy them. That simply wasn't the case in the old Soviet Union. Of course, today anybody can buy a second-hand ZIL, although on a scale of sensible things to do that must rate somewhere below cutting 2in holes into your skull with a rusty saw.

We'll now look at what promises to be the next generation of super-hyper-mega-barges in Russia – and on the face of it they will not disappoint from the bizarreness standpoint. We've already looked at the ZIS and ZIL limousines, and what creative things the designers did to these under the influence of vodka so strong it could power a Soyuz spacecraft. Now, the Russian prime minister, Dmitry Medvedev, has decided it is time the elegance (or do I mean excesses?) of the old mega-barges be resurrected and brought fully up to date. The designers at Slava Saakyan design studios said they wanted to keep the car 'modern, safe, comfortable and to the point', although exactly what that point was remains a mystery. Safety has been enhanced apparently by having no rear window at all; rear windows, it is claimed, attract assassins.

The engine is said to be 'V8 or above', a delightfully vague and maybe vodka-fuelled explanation, so it could well be a V86 for all we know – there's certainly room for one. The design has been kept 'clean', which means it looks like a cross between a stealth bomber, an aircraft carrier and an outsize ironing board. The below photograph shows the vast scale of the latest ZIL.

It is possible the bonnet has been designed to double up as a heli-pad and that the boot is intended to accommodate a small armoured personnel carrier. Currently, just three of these new ZILs exist. I wonder if, like the ZIS 101, they plan to make

an open two-seat version. If so, that would give Porsche and Mercedes something to think about.

The photographs shown here have been taken from the ZIL sales brochure. However, why they need a sales brochure is a mystery given that you cannot actually buy one – you have to be 'granted' one. Oh, and of course currently there are only three of them, so a major marketing campaign seems a little unnecessary.

The Zil Lane to Heaven ... Or Somewhere Else

ZIL lanes were lanes on major highways in Moscow reserved exclusively for top-ranking Soviet officials in their ZILs, the name being revived for exclusive lanes used at various Olympic Games venues. The last of the traditional ZILs was the ZIL-4104, of which just fifty a year were produced for the elite from the late 1970s until around 2002. Weighing in at not far short of 4 tons, even with a 7.7-litre engine, developing 315bhp and enough torque to move the Ural Mountains, it struggled to get much beyond 100mph. They even produced a few 'estate car' versions, like the one shown.

In the end, these found a more specialised role as hearses for the politburo members, handy for whisking them down the ZIL lanes to the pearly gates, or some less desirable 'entrance'. I would imagine the sight of a ZIL-4104 Estate parking outside a politburo member's office window was a less than comforting sight, suggesting the nature of their next 'business' trip.

For its somewhat specialised role, the ZIL-E167 was probably perfect, and hence not bizarre. It was originally designed to cope with the harsh conditions in Siberia and the Urals, as well as the even more challenging conditions of the school run in Kensington and Chelsea. A product of ZIL, this amazing off-roader was built from 1962. Contributing to a certain degree of bizarreness is the apparently quite normal truck cab bolted rather self-consciously on the front. And that is probably where normality ends for the ZIL-E167. Oh, and there seems no obvious way for the driver to reach the cab; maybe he had to be either parachuted in or born there.

It was over 30ft long, a 6x6 with two separate engines, each of 3.5 litres and each producing 180bhp. It could travel on land and water, and no doubt would have made a valiant attempt at flying as well. It had the ability to change tyre pressures on the move to suit the environment. It weighed in at 7 tons and could carry 5 tons of cargo. It could also climb 45-degree slopes, wade through 6ft of water, or 3ft of snow, and climb over 3ft vertical obstacles. It would be hard to think of a better vehicle for the tough school run. Who will argue over a parking space in Kensington if you arrive in an E167? And what traffic warden would attempt to clamp this leviathan when parked on double yellow lines?

There was a downside. It struggled to exceed 2mpg, had a turning circle of around 75 miles (OK, over 40ft), and a fuel tank of 900 litres, meaning it would cost about £1,300 to fill up, even if you could find a petrol station large enough to accommodate it. This may be why some E167s (as on the right) now languish in scrapyards … they just couldn't find a big enough petrol station.

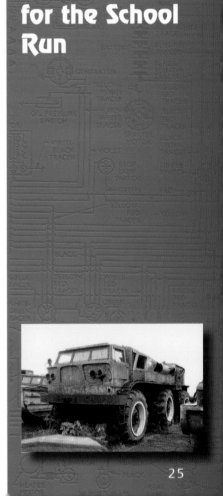

What Sell-By Date?

MORRIS MARINA

Now, the reader is probably curious about a couple of things. Firstly, why is there a picture here of an early 1950s Morris Minor rather than one of a Morris Marina? Secondly, why is the Marina in this book anyway?

Surely the Marina is anything but bizarre? Terminally boring and about as exciting as a wet Sunday afternoon in Scunthorpe, perhaps, but bizarre? Well, in fact there is a very simple and good reason.

The Marina was produced between 1971 and 1980, and was sold in large numbers, but it had one of the lowest survival rates of any post-war car. Of the 807,000 made, only 745 were still in existence in 2006

according to the DVLA, and the number is probably much lower now. So why was it bizarre?

Essentially, the Marina *is* a Morris Minor, a car designed in the 1940s. To be fair to the Marina, it is actually a post-1952 Minor, by which time the car had acquired the British Motoring Corporation A-series engine to replace the previous side valve unit. Although British Leyland had started to make quite sophisticated cars like the Allegro, with the Marina

they decided on safe, conservative, reliable design. So mechanically it is essentially a Morris Minor, even down to the same BMC A-series engines. This does have advantages, though. Many Marinas were broken up to provide spares to restore Morris Minors, which for its day was an excellent little car. So maybe there was some sense in its creation. But maybe it should have been marketed as a Morris Minor Repair Kit, rather than as a car in its own right.

To add to the 'bizarre rating' of the humble Marina, there was a naturally aspirated diesel version which turned out an asthmatic 37bhp, half of which was absorbed by the transmission and a fair bit by the tyres. It was one of the most underpowered cars of the 1970s. At the other end of the scale was the Marina 1.8TC, basically a 1940s Morris Minor with an MGB engine shoehorned into it!

To cope with the extra power they installed super-large powerful brakes, beefed-up suspension, stiffened the chassis and installed power steering. No, all that's a lie; the brakes, suspension chassis and steering were exactly the same as on the basic model. So the 1.8TC was a bit like a demented guided missile, trying to handle loads of wild horse power through farm cart rear suspension, and with a homeopathic dose of braking ability which was scarcely adequate in the 1940s Minor.

As a final bizarre twist, in 1980 a replacement was launched – the Morris Ital – a vastly improved total redesign. No, that's not true either. It was absolutely identical apart from a big plastic bumper and an 'Ital' badge, which made it sound like it was designed by an Italian styling house – which it wasn't. The reheated recipe carried on, or rather lurched on, until 1984 in the UK when it was mercifully allowed to die. However, it was made right up to 1999 in China.

At the beginning of this book I said a bizarre car need not be bad. But in the case of the Marina, it certainly was. It is hard to think of any single redeeming feature of the Marina, beyond providing spares for Minors and having the grace to rust away quickly.

Morris Marina Facts

Produced	1971–80 (nine years too long)
Number sold in UK	807,000 (806,999 too many)
Survivors in UK	745 (in 2006 and counting downwards … fast)
Best model	121bhp, 2.6-litre straight 6 (Australia)
Worst model	1,489cc straight 4 diesel
Best feature	Good as spares for Morris Minor/1000
Worst feature	Everything else, except the door handles (see right)
Most dangerous	1.8TC, an MGB/farm cart crossover
Replacement	Morris Ital (identical except for bumpers & badge)

Heritage: the Marina became, with development, the Hyundai Pony in Korea. Parts of the Marina lived on for ages. The door handles were used in the Allegro, Range Rover, Triumph TR7, Lotus Esprit, Reliant Scimitar and first series Land Rover Discovery. The indicator switchgear has an even more illustrious heritage, finding its way into first the Triumph Stag and then, believe it or not, the Lamborghini Diablo. Don't let it be said the Marina was a totally bad car … the door handles and indicator switchgear were really quite adequate.

The Bugatti 101 Coach is, in many ways, an outstanding vehicle – yet it's certainly bizarre! First, some background.

The Bugatti Type 57 was introduced in 1934 and built up until 1940, when the Second World War stopped production at the Molsheim factory. It had a twin cam 3,257cc straight 8 engine and optional supercharger. Without supercharger it delivered 135bhp, but with supercharger it reached 190bhp. In supercharged form it was definitely the supercar of its day.

I first came across the Type 101 Coach in 1955 when I was just 7 years old. Even at that age I had quite an encyclopaedic knowledge of the car industry and when I saw a picture of the Bugatti Coach I thought it must be

a mistake. Surely Bugatti had ceased production completely in 1940 (well, up until the Veyron, that is). It was only many years later that I discovered the facts.

In 1951 someone found the parts to make more Type 57s, so production restarted. However, only seven, or nine (depending on who you believe, the difference of two possibly being re-bodied pre-war chassis), were made between 1951 and 1965. I am not joking – the last one was completed in 1965, although the others were completed

by 1956. That adds up to exactly half a car per year, which might be a record. Each one had different coachwork and the example shown is one of the two-door coupes, with the only four-door version (the white car) standing behind it.

Why have I dubbed this a 'bizarre' car? Well, under the flashy bodywork is a 1934-designed chassis, complete with semi-elliptic front suspension (yes, front, which means that the first 3 or so feet of the modern-looking

bonnet is actually empty) and quarter elliptic rear suspension. By the time the last car was completed in 1965 the design was 31 years old, and the last Bugatti Coach was launched into a world familiar with E-type Jaguars and Ferrari Superfasts. And it cost an absolute fortune, more than a Ferrari and many times the price of an E-type. Price apart, it would, in chronological terms, be like relaunching the original Austin Allegro (complete with square steering wheel) or the abysmal Morris Marina at the 2006 Motor Show.

Fortunately, eight of the nine survive today (the ninth may also still exist, but this is not certain). The 101 Coach is a unique dinosaur in the motoring world, certainly bizarre but also an epic motor car.

Bugatti Type 57 Facts

Produced	1934–40 (except for 101 Coach)
Number made	710
Engine	(57) 3,257cc twin cam straight 8 135bhp (57SC) 3,257cc twin-cam straight 8 s/charged 200bhp
Top speed	(57) 95mph (57SC) 120mph

The Bugatti 101 Coach was really a Type 57 in drag. In the mid to late 1930s the Type 57 was the real supercar of its day. With a 120mph+ top speed and a 0–60 time well under 10 seconds, it can still hold its own with quite fancy machinery today. The main difference is that, whereas today a Bugatti Veyron can be yours for a trifling £1 million, the last Type 57 Atlantic to be sold fetched an undisclosed amount believed to be US$30–40 million. The last Bugatti 101 Coach to be completed is the one shown below on the right, the famous Exner Ghia car. It's hard to believe that it's essentially a 1934 vehicle, as shown left.

You may be wondering why there are two photos of a 1956 Morris Oxford, one with a slightly updated radiator grille and painted a more modern white? Well, when BMC, as it was, started production of the new Farina models (the ones which were all fins and chrome gloss) in 1957 they sold all the tooling for the Oxford to Hindustan Motors in India. Hindustan Motors started making the Oxford from 1958 and selling it as the Hindustan Ambassador.

From its beginnings in 1956 it has soldiered on and is still made. It's had a bit of a facelift, mainly a new radiator grille and an Isuzu engine replacing the ancient

One of the more recent Hindustan Ambassadors. Not much has changed in forty years.

Morris unit in 1992, but essentially it has remained a 56-year-old design. The 37bhp diesel Ambassador Nova launched in 1989 remains one of the lowest-powered and slowest four-door cars in the world.

The great thing about this car is there are so many of them that there is scarcely a village in India which doesn't have several people who can do anything to it. Take a couple of Ambassador wheel nuts and a door handle to the village blacksmith and he'll rebuild the whole car as new!

It is noisy, ancient, uncomfortable, slow, uneconomical, about as far from 'green' and 'safe' as you can get ... but it is almost impossible not to love it. The car was made available in the UK in 1993, being retro-fitted with 'luxuries' like a heater, ashtray and seat belts. Only a few were sold and the importer went bust. I had a colleague who bought one in 1993. After just one year it looked 37 years old, which in many ways it was.

Hindustan Ambassador, dating from the early 1960s.

31

Hindustan Motors

- Hindustan Motors is based in Uttarpara, India.
- Their first car was a 'recycled' Morris Ten made from 1942 as the Hindustan Landmaster.
- They then acquired the rights to make the Morris MO, the first Minor, and in 1957 purchased the tooling for the Series II Morris Oxford, which became the Ambassador.
- The Ambassador has been in continuous production since 1957, and looks set to go on for many more years.
- There have been five 'generations' of Ambassador, each distinguished by little more than a new grille and headlights.
- There has been just one change of engine, from BMC to Isuzu, in the 1990s, making it the fastest Indian car – this doesn't say a great deal for the competition though.
- A stretched version, the Ambylimo, was produced by Parikh.
- In 1992 there was a radical leap forward with the fitting of seat belts.
- It was imported into the UK in 1993 and again in 2002 at £9,500 with outrageously decadent 'luxury' fittings like reclining seats.
- In 2000 a floor-mounted gear change was introduced.
- It was relaunched as the Avigo in 2004, totally 'revitalised', which seems to have meant in Hindustan Motors terms virtually identical.
- 25% of Hindustan Ambassadors are bought by the Indian government, all in cream.
- It's a tough machine. In 2003 an assassination attempt was made on the chief minister of Andhra Pradesh using a land mine. The Ambi was hardly dented.
- As well as the recycled Morris Oxford, Hindustan Motors made the 1972 Vauxhall Victor FE for a short while, and later a Rover SDI fitted with a 4-cylinder Ferguson tractor engine.

The Toyota Crown may seem like an odd inclusion here as a 'bizarre' car. The photograph shows one of the 18,138 taxis in Hong Kong, 99% of which are all absolutely identical apart from the advertisements on the side.

These 17,957 taxis are red Toyota Crown saloons, with the word 'Comfort' added to the name, presumably to make the customers feel, well, comfortable. They are propelled by rough, noisy, but sturdy 4-cylinder 2-litre engines, running on liquefied water buffalo fart gathered from farms in Hong Kong's New Territories. Well, actually, that's a lie. They are powered by LPG, which chemically is very similar to water buffalo fart but slightly less smelly.

These Toyota Crown Comforts are as roomy as the Albert Hall, as reliable as the sunrise, as robust as an Egyptian pyramid, as economical as a Scottish Presbyterian minister's wife, and as exciting as spending Christmas Day locked in a public toilet in Hartlepool. The inside is very functional with hardwearing vinyl-covered bench seats front and rear. You feel you could happily hose down the inside and have it back plying for passengers after 5 minutes of the most cursory drying off. It is perfectly fit for purpose. So what the heck is it doing here?

Well, the reason lies in its history. Although the Comfort was first introduced in 2001, its origins lie back in the mists of time. Turn the clock back about thirty-three years and the Toyota Crown Custom (6th Series) was the absolute top of the heap of the Toyota car repertoire. A super luxury limousine, techno everything, 148-speed automatic gearbox, furnished like a suite at the Ritz, 32-litre hypo-charged engine, power everything including nail clippers, newspaper page turners in the back, hydraulic cigar trimmers, thought-controlled digital radio ... OK, I exaggerate a bit, but you get my drift. It was real luxury, and at a price. In the UK it cost an absolute fortune. It cost so much very few were sold in Europe. And the bizarre thing is that the Hong Kong taxi is almost exactly that car, but with a few bits removed. Actually, almost everything removed except the bodyshell and name.

It is a bit like finding the 1970s Rolls-Royce Silver Shadow has been relaunched as the 2012 Silver Shadow Super-Fare-Master 4 with a noisy 4-cylinder diesel tractor engine, and all the leather and wood replaced by cheap leatherette and plastic. All the electric gizmos have been removed, the rear axle has been replaced by one from a Victorian ox cart, the windows are worked by a novel sort of handle thing that you turn, and the only additions have been a fare meter and an electric 'for hire' sign on the roof. It just doesn't bear thinking about.

In spite of the Crown taxi being totally fit for purpose, I think its pedigree alone merits its inclusion here as slightly bizarre on the basis of 'sell-by date'. Also, the Toyota Crown Custom Comfort shows every sign of going on for another fifty years and a few more million miles each, by which time its inclusion here should be beyond doubt.

Some cars are born to be bizarre, for various different reasons. The Renault Dauphine enters the hall of bizarreness by being so unremittingly awful you wonder how Renault could ever have considered launching it, and why anybody actually bought one voluntarily. A car cannot be considered bizarre just by being bad, but the bizarre thing about the Dauphine is that 2 million people bought one. It was made from 1956 until 1967. Even when it was launched it was about fifteen years out of date.

The contemporary press reviews say it all:

Time Magazine (2007) The Pulitzer Prize-winning journalist Dan Neil named the Dauphine as amongst the fifty worst cars of all time, and called it 'the most ineffective bit of French engineering since the Maginot Line' and claimed you could actually hear it rusting away.

The Independent (2008) 'As soon as the US market had come to grips with the Dauphine's swing axle manners and useless acceleration, they were pole-axed by its abysmal corrosion record. It would take only one New York winter of driving on salt-strewn roads to give the Dauphine front wings that resembled net curtains.'

Road & Track Magazine They road-tested the Dauphine and found it took 37 seconds to reach 60mph. With performance like that it would be at a disadvantage in a drag race with a combine harvester.

A Renault Dauphine patriotically sporting a small French flag. However, the car was so grossly under-powered the flag would have had to be removed if the miserable beast were to exceed a gentle Gallic amble.

Car Talk (2000) In a survey, the Dauphine was named the ninth worst car of the millennium, noting that it was 'truly unencumbered by the engineering process'.

Popular Science (1958) 'The Dauphine incorporates a bag of annoyances peculiar to itself.'

The most damning comments of all probably came from Renault itself in 1967, who when launching the Dauphine's successor, described it as 'the Renault for people who swore they would never buy another one'.

Renault Dauphine Facts

So was the Dauphine really so bad? Well, let's look at the facts:

- It had just 27bhp from its 845cc engine, only about half that of the lighter Mini.

- It had one of the slowest 0–60 times ever to feature in a post-war road test, and one tester said you needed a calendar rather than a stopwatch.

- Its swing rear axles had no fore/aft location except for the trunnions on the swing arms, which gave 'interesting' handling.

- Its over-steer was so bad the manual advised differential tyre pressures as the best way to control it.

- An engine rebuild after 12,000 miles was not uncommon.

- It looked like something which had dropped out of a cheap Christmas cracker.

- Oh, and perhaps worst of all, it was French.

So the answer is probably … yes.

Bizarre Car Names: Part 1

Names are important, as in any consumer market. For example, would the Jaguar E-type have been such a success had it been called the Jaguar Dinky-Do-Dah Coupe? Of course not, and no manufacturer would give their cars such silly names … or would they?

In a global market, manufacturers need to consider very carefully how names work in different countries and cultures. Throughout the book we will return to this fascinating topic. But as a starter, let's consider the Mitsubishi Shogun. Interestingly, it is known as the Shogun in all Spanish-speaking countries, but elsewhere it is the Pajero. The reason is quite simple. In Spanish *pajero* means 'wanker'. And with so much free movement these days within the EU, quite a lot of Mitsubishi Wankers can be seen in Spain.

Simple Bizarre Overkill

SCAMMELL CONTRACTOR BUS/TRUCK

Many of the vehicles featured in this book are, for one reason or another, ludicrous. And few are more ludicrous than the Scammell Contractor bus/truck. First we need a little basic educational stuff. Let's start with two definitions:

Super Heavy Haulage Tractor *A vast lump of metal with an immensely powerful engine capable of hauling medium-sized countries.*

Bus *A comfortable home from home for gently transporting passengers from A to B along well-made roads without jolting them lest they spill their Horlicks.*

There are two photographs shown, one of a super-heavy haulage tractor and the other of a bus. I will let you work out which is which. One is carrying fifty happy passengers to the shopping precinct. The other is preparing to pull the entire state of Lithuania 2ft to the left before breakfast.

South African State Railways got a tad mixed up and ordered fifteen bus/truck bodies to be built on Scammell Contractor chassis. The bus/truck was apparently used for 'passenger services and light goods delivery'. But, hold on, this bus could tow an oil rig and the QE2 at the same time without even getting into a sweat.

Did the railway company envisage unbelievably fat passengers? Or does 'light' have a different meaning for the South African railways?

It's about 15ft high, half a mile long and weighs around 500 tons empty, or 500.1 tons full of passengers and 'light' goods. It achieved around 1mpg – 99.99% of that just moving the beast itself. Some of the fifteen were produced as pure buses and some as bus/truck combinations. It is, I suppose, a sort of overgrown 'ute', as the Aussies would call it. Surely this is the biggest case of overkill in the entire history of transport?

No doubt its power would come in useful if the bus, whilst taking the workers home, ever encountered a stranded oil refinery or an African state which had somehow ended up in the wrong place. I suppose it did have one advantage. It didn't need to worry about where the roads were; it just drove straight on and created its own. It probably couldn't have taken corners easily anyway.

Scammell Contractor bus/ truck combination; this one resides in the South African Rail Road Museum. (Courtesy of Michael Winkler)

I don't know if any survive other than the one shown, but I imagine it would take a biblical flood to destroy one, so I expect they are still around. They are probably ferrying people up Mount Kilimanjaro 400 at a time, or have been converted to spacecraft launching platforms.

I wonder whether it was all a result of a simple misunderstanding. Maybe someone said on the phone, 'I am looking for a contractor to supply fifteen buses', and it got written down as 'I am looking for a supply of fifteen Contractors as buses', and everyone was too embarrassed to admit the mistake.

Scammell Contractor & Routemaster Comparison

These statistics show how remarkably similar the two vehicles are, and how any normal person might get confused. After all, they are almost exactly the same width and often painted red.

* Standard contractor. South African version 7km, roughly

	Scammell	Routemaster
Number of seats	3	64
Power	450bhp	115bhp
Power per passenger	150bhp	2bhp
Engine	Cummins	AEC
Drive train	6x4	2x1
Designed load/towing capacity	240 tons	4 tons
Length	7,770mm*	12,000mm
Width	2,500mm	2,440mm
Height	2,950mm	4,380mm
Most popular colour	Red	Red

When Jeep and Land Rover first introduced 4x4s they used a similar, simple and robust formula. Take a medieval cart chassis, throw in an unbreakable, very long stroke, 4-cylinder engine (the Standard Triumph 2 litre in the case of the Land Rover; Willys or Ford in the case of the Jeep), add the most basic 'bodywork' fashioned from flat sheets of pop-riveted aluminium, insert the odd canvas seat or two, and there you have it, a good functional vehicle for farmers and the like.

When the Japanese entered the 4x4 market they generally started with the same formula, and it worked well. Only once the manufacturers were well established in the market

did they branch out and include things like 'comfort' and more advanced engines.

Ferruccio Lamborghini was the son of farmers, but he was not interested in the land; he preferred technology. He completed his technical studies in Bologna and soon after was able to put his know-how to the test when during the Second World War he was put in charge of vehicle maintenance in Rhodes, Greece. It was probably due to his experience in the war that once he returned home, he started buying old military vehicles and converting them into tractors, something that Italy desperately needed after the war. The success of this enterprise prompted him to buy a workshop in Cento where, from 1948 onwards, Lamborghini tractors were produced in large numbers.

Now, you might think, given this background, that when he decided to enter the 4x4 market he would launch a pedestrian agricultural product with one of his own tractor engines at the front and a chassis that even Noah might see as a little dated.

But that is not how Ferruccio works. Instead he launched this, the LM.

So, did it have a tractor engine at the front and cartwheel suspension? Not exactly. It was equipped with a 5167cc V12 engine from the Lamborghini Countach, delivering 450bhp and making the LM capable of 0–60 in under 7 seconds. It had full independent suspension and the early models were rear-engined. Later, the engine moved to the front, but the vehicle was so vast the engine could have been almost anywhere, even inside the glove box.

Lamborghini did try to interest the Swiss army into taking the LM as a military vehicle. But I suspect they found no need for a 'jeep' which could potentially traverse their entire country in 6.5 seconds. Though it might just have made military service in enemy-free Switzerland, which is compulsory for all, just a little less boring. I often wonder what old Ferruccio would have produced if he'd turned his hand to hearses, milk floats, invalid carriages and ambulances.

Lamborghini LM

- The first ever four-wheel-drive Lambo.
- It started life as the Cheetah, as a military vehicle, with a limp-wristed Chrysler V8 at the rear.
- During testing the US military managed to totally destroy it.
- Then the prototype LM001 was manufactured but with an AMC V8 engine.
- Lamborghini decided the enormous rear engine layout caused too many handling problems, so introduced a much more 'sensible' front-engined version now with the V12 engine from the Countach.
- After extensive soul searching and debate, this new model was finally called the LM002.
- Now nicknamed the Rambo Lambo, it was deemed too good for US soldiers and instead became a civilian vehicle with leather seats, air con, tinted power windows and a premium stereo mounted in a roof console.
- It became popular with Saudi Sheiks for tearing across the desert, but was never sold to any military. The US army, of course, could not understand the manual gear change.
- Some customers thought the Countach engine was a tad tame, and were able to specify the 7.2-litre marine version of the V12 usually found in Class 1 offshore powerboats.
- The US military couldn't keep their hands off the LM002, and they blew up the one belonging to Uday Hussein to demonstrate the power of a car bomb.

Definition of a Q-Car

The definition of a Q-car on Wikipedia is as follows: 'A Q-car is a Metropolitan Police term for an unmarked police vehicle used for covert patrolling and operations. It is often crewed by plain-clothed officers. A Q-car is usually a high-powered saloon or estate vehicle, fitted with sirens and blue warning lights behind the front grille in order for it to also carry out response duties when necessary. Over time, the term Q-car has evolved to mean any unobtrusively styled high-performance sedan or a performance-tuned model of a car that otherwise appears stock.'

This leads us nicely on to the Lancia Thema 8.32.

By the mid-1980s the Fiat group had begun to rationalise its chassis platforms so that the same body could be used on Fiat, Alfa Romeo and Lancia models. One of the first Fiat group models to pioneer this new platform sharing was the Fiat Croma/Lancia Thema in 1985. As was to be expected, the Lancia version sat at the top of the new range, with a sporty Alfa Romeo version just below it. The Thema came with a choice of 1995cc 4-cylinder (petrol) engine, 2849cc V6 engine or a 2445cc Turbo Diesel. It was a perfectly competent but dull car, if a little too fond of spontaneously disappearing into a heap of rust.

Then some bright spark in the marketing team decided there was room for just one more model in the range. Maybe a 2.5-litre petrol model or an economy 1.8 model? No. They decided to take a perfectly bog-standard-looking Thema bodyshell and shoehorn a 3-litre, 32-valve Ferrari V8 under the bonnet. It makes you wonder why nobody had done it before.

This certainly made the Lancia Thema 8.32, as it was known, a Q-car. The problem was they had taken the concept of Q-car just one step too far.

The only distinguishing feature was '8.32' written on the boot in letters about 2mm high. On my commute to work from Marlow to Reading I used to follow one of these sometimes and needed a high-powered telescope to read the '8.32' sign. Talk about 'Q-cars'. Lancia had decided to stretch the definition to its limits.

It was not a big success. A breathtaking total of nine were sold in the UK. Worldwide, only 2,370 were built over the five years from 1986–91. Why? Well, for one, it cost

£40,000 (yes, £40,000 in 1986! That's around £97,000 in today's terms) and looked just like an ordinary 2-litre Thema costing a quarter of the price. Then you had Ferrari levels of service and repair costs in a car likely to rust away within a few weeks, resulting in depreciation levels almost never seen before in history. Oh, and Ferrari insurance. And Ferrari petrol consumption. And it could only be had in left-hand drive. But the interior was quite nice, if you liked sculptured velour more at home in a pimp's boudoir, and it did have heated seats.

Wouldn't it have been better to buy a real, second-hand Ferrari? Or even a bog-standard 2-litre Thema and blow the remaining £30,000 (£72,000 in today's money) on booze and birds? The concept of a Q-car can be taken a tad too far.

Hummer Facts

The Hummer story started in 1984 when AM General first produced the gargantuan High Mobility Multipurpose Wheeled Vehicle (or HMMWV) for the US military. It was about the size of Massachusetts, weighed about the same as the Statue of Liberty, and was powered by engines ranging from a puny 6.2-litre V8 diesel up to a 4,580-litre V96 triple stage supercharged engine, running on pure rye whiskey and space dust (OK, I exaggerate a little).

Although it was only 15ft long, it was over 7ft wide and weighed around 3 tons. It could, fully loaded, achieve the massive top speed of 55mph. At that speed it had such a dense, smoky exhaust that it could create its own smokescreen. It could tow entire countries and flatten quite substantial hills. It was definitely fit for purpose.

There was also a civilian version, the H1, which was the same size and powered by Detroit diesels ranging from 6.2 litres to 6.5 litres. Realising that most US states were not large enough to accommodate more than half a dozen they created a smaller version based on the GM GMT820 truck, and after months of discussion came up with the exciting and original name of H2.

The bottom line is that the H2 is merely a GM truck in fancy dress, and not very pleasant fancy dress at that – more like a scary Halloween costume.

The original Hummer is the one on the left. The H2 is the one on the right. Yes, it's the one which looks like a Tonka toy.

So where does this leave us in the most ludicrous car stakes? Well, one genius decided to make a stretch-limo version. It was actually the brainchild of a limo business called Style Limousines (not Hummer), but that doesn't make it any less bizarre. This 16-seat, 4-axle monster

(Courtesy of Danny Cawley, Style Limousines)

comes complete with a disco bar, eight flat-screen TVs, a 12,000-watt music system, 20ft mirrored ceiling, and must be the least fit-for-purpose vehicle in the world. Remember, the name derived from High Mobility Multipurpose Wheeled Vehicle – high mobility it certainly is not (it cannot go around 90% of street corners); multipurpose? No. But it is a wheeled vehicle, with maybe a sag in the middle. So I suppose they could call it the Low Mobility Single Purpose Slightly Saggy Wheeled Vehicle, or

Style Limousines show the Yanks what a Hummer really should look like. (Courtesy of Danny Cawley, Style Limousines)

LMSPSSWV for short. But, all credit to Style Limousines, it does have a certain presence!

Oh, and the limo business concerned decided this Hummer was simply too sensible and have now constructed a stretched Ferrari, the world's fastest stretch limo, albeit at a modest 25ft long.

We are all accustomed to seeing stretch limos converted from large saloons, often American ones, but also from Rolls-Royce and Jaguars, and even Volvos and Fords. We are also now familiar with the stretched Hummer. But the prize for the most bizarre stretch limo must surely go to the stretched Trabant shown here.

Not exactly the world's longest, at just 16ft, it wins the accolade on the grounds of being totally bonkers. I must confess, though, I rather like it. But the 'stretch' is more a stretch of the imagination!

The World's Most Bizarre Stretch Limo

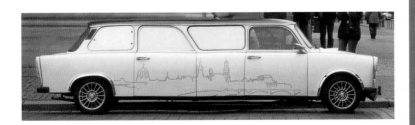

Now for a truly bizarre solution to a simple logistics problem. A certain John Dodd was a mechanic who specialised in servicing Epsom automatic transmissions at customer bases across Europe. Obviously he needed transport to get him from A to B, and to carry the essential tools. So what did the ingenious Mr Dodd do? He decided the obvious and best solution was to install a 27-litre Rolls-Royce Merlin aero engine into a tailor-made chassis, use the bodywork of a Ford Capri, and fit a football pitch-sized bonnet made of fibreglass. The Beast, as it became known, was built by Paul Jameson.

From the rear the Beast looked almost normal, so it must have given quite a shock to anyone overtaking when they realised it was actually a quarter of a mile long, although I suspect it was not overtaken very often. The six exhaust pipes were the only clue from behind that this was far from an ordinary set of wheels.

The Beast was once listed in the *Guinness Book of Records* as the world's most powerful road car. The engine came from a Boulton Paul Balliol training aircraft which gave 1,262hp (941kW) at 8,500ft (2,600m). The supercharger was removed before fitting the engine to the car, so it *only* delivered a puny 850hp (630kW), which really is a little on the low side for a mobile mechanic's car. However, it developed enough torque to bend the local gravitational field. It was reputed to have reached 200mph on a German autobahn. What it would

A full-length view of the Beast. Or is it Del Boy's banger on steroids? (Images courtesy of B.J. Deller)

An under-bonnet shot of the Beast's mighty 27-litre Merlin engine. (Courtesy of B.J. Deller)

have been like if Dodd had left the supercharger in place we will never know.

The Beast was not without its problems. With an engine weighing over 1 ton and no power steering, it certainly preferred straight roads. Overall, it would return around 2mpg, although Dodd discovered he could dramatically increase this to 5–6mpg by turning the engine off going downhill, albeit at the expense of the power-assisted braking. With a tank of just 26 gallons, range was definitely on the restricted side at around 52 miles, or up to 156 miles downhill.

With the front suspension from a 1960s Austin 110 Westminster, rear suspension from a Jaguar XJ12, and a homemade chassis restraining the 60-year-old Merlin's power, it was reported to have 'interesting' handling.

Clearly Jameson, the car's builder, decided the Beast was not bizarre enough for him, because in the mid-1970s he designed a second Merlin-powered car. This one had six wheels – two in front and four driven at the rear – a mid-engined layout and it retained the supercharger. It apparently resides in a museum in Sweden, no doubt shackled to the wall struggling to get out, as any self-respecting Beast should.

The Beast itself also still exists and can be found in Spain. Unfortunately, however, John Dodd has passed away and the Beast is said to also be in poor health, and may never run on the roads again.

The Merlin-Powered Cars

The Beast wasn't the only Merlin-powered car. There were at least nine others:

- In the 1970s Rolls-Royce collector Nicholas Harley, of London, installed a Merlin in a 1931 Phantom II chassis. The engine consumed 100 gallons of petrol every hour, regardless of what speed it was doing!

- In 1953 the Smalldean Spitfire Special was built by Michael Wilcock, owner of the Smalldean Garage in Worthing. This was based on two Daimler Dingo Scout Car chassis welded end to end and used a supercharged Merlin delivering 1,600bhp.

- A 1955 Chevrolet Bel Air Sports Coupe has been converted to Merlin power, and is nicknamed the Final Objective.

- In 1970 Paul Jameson, who had built the Beast, made a second Merlin car which was six-wheeled and mid engined. It had full two-stage supercharging.

- In the 1990s Charlie Broomfield from Lincolnshire built a Merlin into a Rover SDI. It delivers a staggering 1,550ft-lb of torque at just 1,600rpm, so gears are a pure luxury. To be fair, the engine is actually a Merlin-derived Meteor tank engine. Charlie wouldn't reveal the full cost, apart from two marriages.

- At least four others have existed, including one from Petersen Engineering with a Merlin on a stretched 4.25-litre Bentley chassis, the custom-made Handlye Special, a US street rod with a Meteor engine, and even a Land Rover.

Now for a very modern freak – the K.A.Z. (Keio Advanced Zero-Emission Vehicle) from Keio University in Japan. Let's go straight to the looks … I'll give you a few minutes to stop laughing. It's not from the set of a kids' space cartoon, it's for real:

1 For top speed it'll knock the pants, or boxster shorts, off a Porsche Boxster.

2 Over the standing start quarter mile it can thrash a Ferrari 328 so convincingly that it's finished before the 328's rear wheels have crossed the starting line.

3 It develops 590bhp, which in the technical language of the design engineers is known as 'a f*****g lot'.

4 It can carry eight people, their luggage, their pets, most of their immediate relatives, a few of their neighbours and most of their furniture, and still have room inside for them all to fall around laughing as well, even at close to 200mph.

Oh, I forgot to mention, it is a 'limousine' – a limousine which looks like a cross between a ballistic missile and two large people carriers mating. And it's powered by rather a lot of 3.75-volt batteries, apparently. Another mystery is distinguishing the front from the back. I think the K.A.Z. is something only the Japanese could have made.

But that is not the end of the story. Having decided that the K.A.Z. was quite ridiculous at 22ft long, with eight wheels and producing 590bhp, the same team decided it was time to return to planet Earth and design something sensible that could be put into production. So they designed the ELIICA (Electric Lithium Ion Car). This is a much more down-to-earth car, as the fact box shows. It is clearly aimed at more of a mass market.

They plan two models, a 'speed' model and an 'acceleration' model. The speed model will exceed 230mph and the acceleration model will reach 62mph in well under 4 seconds. Maybe they should design a third, Nutcase model, which does both. Some things can only happen in Japan. It's probably best those things stay there as well.

Eliica Facts

Produced	2004–??
Number planned	200
Target price	$255,000
Power	640bhp
Maximum speed	230mph (speed model)
0–62 time	4.0 seconds
Drive train	8x8 via wheel hub electric motors

Steering	Four-wheel steering
Number of seats	8
Length	5.1m
Weight	2,400kg
Batteries	320
Charge time	10 hours
Battery replacement cost	£50,000

Overkill on Two Wheels

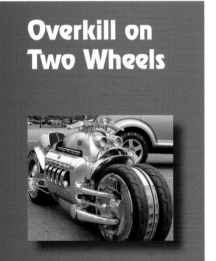

In 2003, the Tomahawk came into being. The 8.3-litre V10 engine is also the chassis, the suspension front and rear being bolted directly to the crankcase. It has two wheels front and rear, each of which can move independently, and is really neither a bike nor a car. More of a … thing!

With 500bhp in a 'vehicle' weighing not much more than a sliced loaf, and most of that weight being the engine, its performance could be described as 'mildly interesting'. Dodge engineers initially worked out it should reach 60mph in around 2 seconds, and have a top speed of around 420mph, but revised it down to 300mph after a strong cup of coffee or two. The only problem was nobody could be found who was brave enough to take it above 100mph. Although not street legal, thank God, and being described by Dodge as not so much a vehicle more a 'rolling sculpture', nine were made and sold for around $555,000 each.

In many ways it was fortunate they decided to give the Tomahawk twin wheels front and rear, as this gave it natural stability. If it had had just two wheels, and had toppled over, it would have required a substantial crane or two to get it upright again.

The Moke (which actually means donkey) was designed by Sir Alec Issigonis and was initially intended as a military vehicle. It was basically a stripped-down Mini; indeed, so stripped down that when first launched it not only had no doors or windows, but all the seats except the driver's were optional extras, which already made it slightly bizarre! It started life with an 848cc engine at the front. It was not a big hit with the military because of limited ground clearance.

So what did BMC do to make it more attractive to the army? Increase the ground clearance, perhaps? No. Remember, this was the company which introduced the Allegro around the same time. They decided to launch the 'Twinni' Moke, with engines at both front and back and four-wheel drive … well, in the sense that each engine independently drove its own two wheels. To make it even more interesting, and thereby truly bizarre, they decided not to link the two engines together. It retained two separate gear levers, two ignition keys, but just one accelerator. So, if you wished, by removing the flimsy linkage between the two gear sticks you could be on full throttle with the front engine in forward gear and full throttle on the rear engine in reverse. It had no rear seats and absolutely no place to carry anything except the driver and his one passenger, somewhat limiting its military application. Given the combined 1,696cc capacity in a car weighing about as much as an A4 envelope, performance was, potentially at least, lively.

Although the bizarre Twinni Moke was a complete flop with the military (600 were nevertheless made), the single-engine Moke went on to be quite successful as a cult car, and also a vehicle good for holidaymakers to hire in hot countries.

Looking back, the choice of the name 'Moke', or donkey, seems uncannily appropriate, especially if prefixed by a word like 'lame'. Oh, and just one final detail. As already mentioned, one of the problems

The Twinni Moke, showing the second engine in the back and the absence of rear seats as a result.

of the Moke for military use was the almost total absence of ground clearance, and the bodywork would scrape on the ground with just the slightest persuasion. That in itself might not have been too bad on a muddy battlefield, but unfortunately the broad 'side pod' or box making up the passenger's side of the chassis is actually … the fuel tank. Not quite so comforting for tourists negotiating rough, rock-strewn tracks in some remote countryside in a far-off country.

ARIEL ATOM

The Ariel Atom is a current production model which most certainly deserves inclusion as a bizarre car under the 'overkill' heading. The Atom began life as a student project at Coventry University. It was at first known as the LSC, or Lightweight Sports Car. Further developed by the university, with funding from various sources including TWR and British Steel, the Ariel Motor Company was created. The car had its first full public viewing at the 1996 Motor Show at the NEC.

The Atom is bizarre firstly because it has an exo-skeleton, with the chassis on full view outside the 'innards', rather akin to a lady tucking her dress into her tights. But what makes the car truly bizarre is its

technical specification. Engines range from a 2.0-litre Honda K20A1 i-VTEC delivering 245bhp to a supercharged version giving a lame 300bhp to a truly bonkers V8 model which churns out a modest 500bhp. And all this in a car which weighs about the same as two bags of sugar ... well, actually 981lb. But that means, in the case of the V8, a power to weight ratio of around 1,300bhp/tonne.

The 'low'-powered 'hairdresser' 4-cylinder models take a leisurely 3 seconds to reach 0–60, almost enough time to complete a full perm, and run out of steam at a paltry 155mph. Not too bad for a car, but brilliant for a collection of scaffolding poles, a couple of sheets of bent aluminium and a seat strapped to a Honda engine. The totally bonkers V8 accelerates so quickly they have yet to design a stopwatch capable of timing it. Its 0–60 has to be estimated by computer simulation, and is believed to be something around 5.6 milliseconds.

Of course, the Atom comes at a price, ranging from £30,000 for the un-supercharged 'girlie' 4-cylinder to

£45,000 for the 'real man's' V8. But for this you do get quite a high-spec car loaded with 'extras' ... no doors, no windows, no windscreen, no roof, no radio, no heater, no boot, and, well, no bodywork. It works out at £46/lb, more than a Rolls Phantom and twice a top-grade Aberdeen Angus prime steak. But it is road legal, unlike the beef.

The Atom also holds a unique record, for the highest speed attained by a road car indoors, measured at the NEC. In the process it was still spinning its wheels at 70mph whilst it struggled to control its power, weighing as it does about the same as a butterfly. It is also famous for hideously distorting Jeremy Clarkson's face on *Top Gear* when he took the Atom round the test track. It actually made Clarkson look almost handsome.

It's a shame they haven't yet produced a stretched limousine version, an Atom van or maybe an Atom hearse – that would give an entirely new meaning to the term 'in a hurry to meet his maker'. Maybe one day Atom will pull its finger out and make a truly quick car!

Bizarreness on an Imperial Chinese Scale

GEELY GE LIMOUSINE

We all recognise the Chinese as the true kings of counterfeit products. Just think of the fake Rolexes, fake Prada handbags, fake Louis Vuitton suitcases, fake baby milk etc. Well, in the case of the Geely GE Limousine, some enterprising car executives took fakery to the extreme, putting the Geely GE Limousine right at the epicentre of bizarreness.

OK, not too hideous perhaps, but even the most generous Sinophile must admit it looks more than a tad like a Rolls-Royce Phantom, even though Geely vehemently denied it was in any way a copy. They say any similarity was pure coincidence, and I'm sure we believe them.

In reality, there are some big differences. Firstly, the Geely costs around £30,000, about one-eighth of the cost of a Phantom in the UK, and around one-twentieth of a real Phantom once shipped to China with import duties and freight paid. The second difference is that whilst the Phantom is a superb, quality, luxury motor, the Geely is complete crap. Thirdly, and most significantly, the Geely is a three-seater. Yes, that was not a misprint; it was designed, all 20ft of it, to carry just one single passenger in the rear!

The single passenger is ensconced in the rear on what can only be described as an imperial throne. To add to the regal atmosphere, the headlining in the rear 'throne room' is an illuminated star-studded panorama, and the 'throne' can be raised up for the proletariat to get a better view of their 'emperor'. Maybe the Geely is the inevitable long-term result of the strict one-child policy in China.

Now, whilst this might be great for the aspiring 'emperor', I do

wonder what he is supposed to do with his wife and family, assuming his outrageous narcissism has not already driven them away. The boot is quite large, I suppose, and a few breathing holes could easily be introduced.

Not surprisingly, Rolls-Royce took great exception to the design and the Geely was remodelled. But that was not a great success. The new design doesn't just look ridiculous; it looks ridiculous and hideously ugly. On the plus side, however, in the new Geely the single rear imperial throne has been replaced with twin thrones for the emperor and his empress. A big step forward for equality, at least.

The Chinese car industry is nothing if not competitive. Just as you can buy different fake Rolexes, so you can buy different fake Rolls-Royces in China. When Hongqi discovered Geely were making a fake Rolls, they decided to jump on the band-rickshaw, as it were, and produce their own.

There were some subtle differences in approach, however. Whereas the original Geely was just hideously ugly, the design gurus at Hongqi used their undeniable genius to make the HQD monumentally hideous even by intergalactic standards. It's the sort of car which might give you bad dreams or send dogs in the street fleeing for cover. The radiator grille was clearly inspired by one of those retro 1930s-style multi-slice toasters you find in upmarket hotels, whilst the headlamp assembly looks like a cross between a transparent diver's helmet and a goldfish bowl on steroids.

Secondly, while the Geely costs around £30,000, the price of the Hongqi was set at a staggering $1.2 million (or around £800,000). It does come with a fairly sophisticated

6-litre 402bhp V12 which is entirely, 100%, 'in-house' designed and developed (they say). Of course, any similarity to the identical 6.7-litre 453bhp V12 Rolls-Royce engine is pure coincidence, and just as with Geely, of course, we believe them.

But what makes the Hongqi a true candidate for bizarredom, beyond its price and nightmare-inducing

appearance, is its underpinnings. Underneath, the chassis is actually a Toyota Landcruiser Prado. No, that is not a joke; this $1.2 million luxury limousine really is based on a Japanese jeep. I expect that in the off-road stakes the Hongqi can hit the real Rolls and the Geely for six, no doubt useful for the school run in suburban Shanghai.

In my book, spending the price of a large Home Counties detached house on a tarted-up Toyota Landcruiser guaranteed to scare dogs and cats sounds about as sensible as … well, I really can't think of anything comparable, but its inclusion here is well deserved.

The long wheelbase Hongqi CA770. Note the curvature of the earth. (autosohu)

A Car Inspired by the Great Wall of China

The Hongqi CA770 Red Flag started life in 1963 and was a predecessor of the Hongqi HQD. It reflected closely the specification of the contemporary Russian ZIL, and had a virtually identical 5.7-litre V8 engine, developing 220bhp, and a 2-speed automatic box. However, in the well-established tradition of the Chinese car industry, Hongqi dismissed any similarities with the ZIL as 'pure coincidence'. The standard Hongqi was no mini, at 19ft long, 7ft wide and 2.5 tons. It struggled to return 12mpg, ran out of steam at 98mph, and with a fuel tank of just 20 gallons its range was distinctly limited. Hongqi actually means 'red flag', so the name used by westerners is actually Red Flag Red Flag – a bit like having a car called the Rolls-Royce Rolls-Royce.

It appears as though the design guys at Hongqi caught sight of a photograph of part of the Great Wall and decided to make a car that could be seen from the moon. Also, it looks as though two teams started work, one from each end, taking their design cues from the Wall, both thinking they were designing the front. They ended up with something almost symmetrical and around 50ft long.

The photographs shown here were taken at a motor show in Shanghai. I don't know whether the car was driven into the hall or whether it was assembled in situ. The inside of the car looks rather like the reception area in a cheap 1960s brothel in suburban Beijing (not that I would know, of course).

The last CA770s were made in 1983 after a twenty-year run. I presume any old spare Red Flags could be used to patch up parts of the Great Wall.

The nice domestic interior of the CA770. (autosohu)

54

Bizarre Car Names: Part 2

Back to bizarre car names, and here is a sample of some branding errors:

Mazda LaPuta	A pleasant little 3-door hatchback with a diminutive 659cc engine, but a problem in Spain because *laputa* in Spanish means 'whore'.
Nissan Moco	The Moco is a 5-door mini MPV, also sold as the Suzuki MR Wagon. But, once again, a problem in Spain – *moco* means 'snot'.
Buick LaCrosse	Buick's best-selling luxury 'sedan' has a name derived from the game of lacrosse. Unfortunately, take your LaCrosse over the border from the US into Canada and drive to the French area of Quebec, and suddenly your Buick's name means either 'masturbating teenagers' or 'cheating' – take your pick!
Opel Ascona	Now, what is it with the Spanish and car names? In both Spain and Portugal the name of Opel's medium-size saloon, known in the UK as the Vauxhall Cavalier, is a word used to describe female genitalia.
Ford Probe	Well, what can you say about the name Ford chose for their sporty model? 'Would you like to see my Probe?'
Mercedes-Benz Vito	This also means female genitalia in Sweden.
Ford Kuga	In Croatian, *kuga* means the 'plague'.

During the later stages of the typical degree level course in automotive design, students learn some highly technical principles about car design. One of the more advanced aspects of car design, maybe not fully understood by the layman, is that cars should have a front and a back. This is quite a difficult concept for most people to grasp, even some seasoned car designers.

Take the Chery QQMe. Well, take it after you've stopped laughing at its bizarre name. For the front, the designer clearly wanted to give the car a sort of cute appearance, apparently to appeal to the female buyers. Then the designer suddenly remembered his old course work and realised the car also needed a back. Maybe it was late on Friday afternoon and he was running out of time; or maybe he just thought the front so irresistibly cute that he decided to make the back exactly the same.

Of course, in reality the front and back are completely different. The front has two windscreen wipers, the back has just one. You would have to be completely stupid not to notice that. And it is clear that the front is saying 'hello' whereas the back is keeping its lips sealed (maybe out of embarrassment).

The front of the Chery QQMe ... or is it the rear? (autosohu)

The rear of the Chery QQMe ... or is it the front? (autosohu)

Black Tyres are So Yesterday!

The Chinese are noted for their entrepreneurship, and I can only presume that one day a tyre designer, assuming there are such things, was wandering through the streets of Beijing when he was struck by a brainwave: 'Why, in our great country of China, do we make do with decadent black western-style car tyres when we could have bright red ones to reflect our magnificent imperial past?' And so came about a fashion revolution in rubber, which to be honest does sound a tad kinky.

The product is called 'Rainbow' and the possibilities are endless. Red tyres for the fire service, green for bearded sandal wearers, flashing blue for the police, a fetching pink for the gay community, white tyres for black people fed up with having to drive on black tyres with the implied racial subjugation, and so on. A different colour for each wheel, perhaps? Think how much easier that would make it when you go to Kwik Fit; all you'd have to say is 'please change the pink and green ones, the cerise and turquoise ones are fine'. How long before we see Hello Kitty, Peppa Pig or SpongeBob SquarePants tyres for kids' pedal cars? The day may come when women can choose their car tyres to match their dress.

There are two slight technical drawbacks to these new tyres, however. Normal tyres aren't black just because some car designers have a weird fetish with the colour. They're black because of the carbon which gives them all their strength and longevity. Take the black stuff away and … well, it doesn't bear thinking about. Secondly, it would be a bit like that old BT advertisement: 'yes, we have all the tyres in all the sizes in all the colours.' Kwik Fit had better look at increasing the size of their fitting centres by a factor of ten.

Delegates at the 24th Chinese People's Congress on Advanced Polychromatic Automotive Rubber Based Circular Propulsion Aid Modules present the latest concepts in coloured tyres. (bandao.cn)

This morning I was cleaning out our refrigerator (my wife having explained to me how much I would love to do it), and when I removed the egg storage tray it had two slices of cucumber adhering to it from yesterday's salad. For no reason I can think of, apart from some sort of divine intervention, I took a photograph of it. Later in the day I was researching for this book when I came across the photographs of the Tang Hua stand showcasing their electric cars at the Detroit Motor Show. I now know where the inspiration for their sensational four-seat car came from.

It is clear that the Chinese car designer has similar problems with cross-contamination in his fridge, except his clearly has bright yellow internal fitments. In fact, Tang Hua do a range of cars, all of them bright banana yellow (except the ones which are electric blue). The range includes an egg cup lookalike and one with a passing resemblance to an actual banana.

The specification of these cars is guaranteed to set the world alight.

The electric motors deliver an earth-moving 4kW, which is slightly more than my electric toothbrush. This propels the vehicles to a breathtaking 31mph – slow for a car but fast for a banana or toothbrush. The range is claimed to be around 93 miles, so it is unlikely many Chinese will go on holiday in their electric bananas.

Oh, I forgot to add, the motorised egg rack is also amphibious, earning the nickname the Detroit Fish. For me it has rather too many holes to be a boat.

Bizarre Car Names: Part 3

A few more priceless branding 'bloomers' …

Kia Picanto	A problem in Brazil – *pica* means 'penis' and *canto* means 'singing'. Mmm, a singing cock?
Citroen Saxo	In Turkish *saxo* means 'oral sex'.
Hyundai Getz	In Hungarian *getz* means 'sperm'.
Alfa MiTo	In French *mito* sounds just like the word for 'pathological liar'.
Skoda Laura	In Hindi *laura* means 'penis'.
Hyundai Santa Fe	In Arabic *santa fe* means 'it smells bad'.
Daihatsu Scat	The Scat, also known in some markets as the Taft (now that's nearly as daft!), was a small jeep-type vehicle similar to the Suzuki Jimny (yes, nearly as silly again) and also sold by Toyota as the Blizzard. To choose a name which also means 'animal excrement' shows the imagination of some marketing guys. The Scat was replaced by the Rugger … I'll say no more.
Honda Fitta	This time it's Scandinavia where the manufacturer might encounter a little consumer resistance. In Swedish and Norwegian *fitta* is a vulgar name for certain parts of the female genitalia.
Honda That's	Yes, that was a real car. The Honda That's was a rather strange 'cube' of a car, but what makes it really bizarre is the sort of conversation it could have initiated: 'I've just bought a Honda That's.' 'A Honda that's what?' 'No, just a Honda That's!' 'Yes, but that's what?' … and so it could go on forever.

Misunderstanding the Market

ALFA ROMEO ARNA

I think there are maybe three main groups of car buyers in the world:

1 Those who want the excitement of a highly strung and temperamental Italian engine, revving to 15 billion rpm and surviving maybe six months at best, clothed in an Italian body so beautiful you want to have children with it.

2 Those who crave the mechanical dependability and reliability of the most boring Japanese offering of all time, with the styling appeal of a cheap plastic toilet brush.

3 Those who would like the mechanical dependability and reliability of a Nissan Cherry but enclosed in the glamour and beauty of the Alfa SZ.

Well, bad news. The third offering does not exist. Sorry, but life can be tough.

But there is a fourth group – those who desperately crave the stylistic appeal of a plastic toilet brush coupled with the mechanical reliability of a stick of aged, sweating Semtex explosive. These people are in luck, because there is an answer: the Alfa Romeo Arna. This could be one of the most unnecessary cars of all time.

Nissan was having problems with import quotas into Europe, so it created a partnership with a European manufacturer for a joint venture. Nissan would export parts of the car for final assembly in Europe, with other bits supplied by a European partner. Over to the famous marketing guys. They thought it would be just a hog-whimperingly super idea to combine

Nissan Cherry – all the style of a toilet brush.

the soul-numbing body and style of the Nissan Cherry with the glass-like fragility of an Alfa Romeo boxer engine. What a wheeze! A car completely devoid of any positive features but packed to the roof rack with negative ones. And they decide to call it the 'Arna', something to do with Alfa Romeo Nissan Arseholes or something. Alfa Romeo Anus would have been better.

Now, doesn't it look so (yawn) sexy? So (another yawn) different from a bog-standard Nissan Cherry? Well, no, and that was the problem. It looked as exciting as a suitcase; actually less exciting because a suitcase at least has big handles on the side and promises exotic travel. The Arna promised a rainy, cold, February night in in Rochdale. It was total crap, and unnecessary crap, because no one actually wanted one.

The result was such a storming success it lasted about three months and attracted around four buyers. Does anyone know anybody who actually bought one? It was a car that never had any right to exist. Luckily, it rusted away surprisingly quickly for a Japanese car; that is the one area where they truly captured the Alfa spirit.

The super-sexy Alfa Romeo Arna, the car all red-blooded men really lust after.

Alfa Romeo SZ – a car you want to have children with.

A Q-car is a car which looks ordinary but packs an unexpected punch. The perfect example is the Lance Thema 8.32, a boringly bog-standard Lancia rust-bucket with a fragile Ferrari V8 engine under the bonnet, covered earlier in this book. So what is the opposite of a Q-car? A car which looks like it offers everything but is a total let-down in all areas?

The Simca 1100 was, in its day, a great little car. It combined front-wheel drive, a transverse engine, a five-door bodyshell, excellent handling and first-rate value for money. It looked humble and modest. Not exciting, but competent and reliable – and thousands bought one.

It was the marketing guys who cocked it all up. They saw Land Rover dominating the off-road 4x4 market and the Far Eastern manufacturers increasingly gaining a share. So they decided to launch their own 4x4: a butch, outdoor, manly vehicle which could conquer mountains whilst carrying 50 tons of straw bales, forty SAS soldiers and their kit, and two fully grown elephants in the back. Well, not quite.

They decided instead to take the Simca 1100 van, saw off the back bodywork, replace it with a cheap fibreglass workman's hut, add a

searchlight and a few bull bars and things, and launch it as the Simca Matra Rancho. It looked great. But being only front-wheel drive, and with about as much power as a second-hand hedge trimmer, it battled to drive over empty crisp packets, never mind go off road. The name 'Rancho' sounded butch enough and conjured up images of tough cowboys on unforgiving prairies, but the car was in reality a limp-wristed wimp in a posing pouch stuffed full of tissues.

OK, let's forget the ludicrous name for one minute and look at the background to this car. We have already covered the Simca Matra Rancho, which in style terms was twenty years ahead of its time. And such was the Rancho's impact that Heuliez, the coachbuilder who had developed the 1100 van and the Rancho for Simca, had the smart idea of building a 'lifestyle' version of the Talbot-SIMCA 1100 based on the pick-up version. This model was intended to give aspiring Rancho owners the opportunity to own a cheaper lifestyle version of the 1100. The result was the Talbot Wind. And in the brochures it looked very stylish indeed.

Now the Wind was not a success. Why? Well, maybe there are three lessons here:

- Having made a mistake once with the Rancho, for God's sake don't make the same mistake again.
- It was bad enough with a macho name like Rancho, so don't compound the sin by calling it the Wind – were the Flatulence or the Fart considered as alternative names?
- Don't remove the one useful bit of the old Rancho (the fibreglass working men's hut), because once the car has rusted away (which takes around six weeks), the hut can at least find a useful life on an allotment somewhere.

If the Wind was a 'lifestyle' car it is perhaps not surprising that so few people hankered after its lifestyle. It may be symptomatic that I could only find two photographs of a Wind. Maybe photographers were too embarrassed to be seen even shooting the vehicle.

An 'action' photo of the Talbot Wind.

The inclusion of the Austin Allegro may seem a little odd at first. It was a relatively sophisticated car for its time, and in spite of being about as attractive as a rusty coal scuttle, it sold well in its peak years. Indeed, during its first six years it steadily held a place in the top five selling new cars, and around 1,000 Allegros are still registered with the DVLA. However, the Allegro merits the label 'bizarre' for a number of reasons.

Firstly, some truly inspired genius in the design department of British Leyland thought it would be a real hoot to equip their new car with a square steering wheel, on the basis that it allowed more room for the driver's legs. The same genius clearly failed to grasp the simple concept of

turning corners, whereupon there was less room for the driver's legs. They didn't actually call it 'square', but coined the wonderful term 'quartic'. The square steering wheel was not a success and was soon dropped. The word 'quartic' was not a success and was soon dropped; pity, really, as I think Trafalgar Quartic has a sort of special ring to it that Trafalgar Square doesn't. And we could have replaced all roundabouts with squareabouts to make Allegro drivers feel at home.

It may be a surprise to learn that British Leyland resisted the temptation to go one step further, with a *triangular* steering wheel. This would have given even more room for the driver's lower limbs, but might have posed a rather more embarrassing and painful risk in the event of a frontal impact pushing the steering column rearwards and downwards. But perhaps the most bizarre thing about the Allegro is something you cannot actually see. Apparently, its drag coefficient was lower when it was reversing than when it was going forward. If they had installed the gearbox the

wrong way round I presume fuel economy would have been boosted significantly by reversing everywhere.

Two other features of the design deserve a mention here. Firstly, although it looked like a hatchback, it wasn't, which must have caused a lot of confusion in later years when cars that looked like hatchbacks generally were hatchbacks. Secondly, the Allegro used the ancient BMC A-series engine which was never intended for front-wheel drive cars. Once the engine was mounted on top of the transmission, as was necessary for the front-wheel drive Allegro, the engine sat so high they had to incorporate an enormous bulge in the bonnet.

Finally, there was one other feature which made the Allegro truly bizarre, but only within the context of British Leyland. At the time, most BL cars would rust away entirely within minutes of being shown a damp paper tissue at 50m. The bizarre thing about the Allegro was that it didn't rust; possibly the only good thing about a car that was otherwise a complete load of shit! So quite a few survive.

Allegro Facts

- The Allegro was made by British Leyland, only under the Austin name, from 1973 until 1983.
- In 1974 and 1975 it was also produced in Italy as the Innocenti Regent, an anagram of which is Not Nice Entering, which may not be significant.
- The car was also assembled in Belgium from knockdown kits, which must have made it one of the most exciting things going on in Belgium at the time, or any time for that matter.
- A total of 642,350 were made.
- Most had the old BMC A-series engine first introduced in 1951, so this venerable lump was already 21 years old when the first Allegro was made.
- In 2008 a poll amongst readers of *The Sun* rated the Allegro as the worst British car of all time.
- An early edition of *What Car?* included an interview about the Allegro with one BL dealership. The staff at the dealership thought the interview was about the Austin 1100/1300, and made a comment about serious corrosion problems in the rear sub-frame. This non-problem with the Allegro was reported in the magazine, doing nothing for the Allegro's reputation.
- In 1975 the series 2 was launched, with a major restyling … well, actually just the grille and reversing light were changed.
- In 1979 there came the Allegro 3, but the car was already tired, and a bit of cosmetic tarting-up did little for sales.

Car designers take cues from many things when styling a new car. However, the Minissima, designed by William Towns, the man behind the Aston Martin DBS and Lagonda, deserves inclusion here as possibly the only car whose design was based on a wedge of Stilton cheese. Note that it even has the rind on top! All it really needs now is a 'best before' label.

Given Mr Town's previous track record, can we see links between the Minissima and the Astons? I suppose if you were totally pissed in a dark room and squinted at the car by candlelight whilst having your attention diverted by a back massage from a semi-naked Thai masseuse, you might see the resemblance between the Astons and the Minissima.

No? Well they both have wheels, a number plate and a windscreen wiper. What more do you want? And although 75cm shorter than the Mini it still has four seats. But it has just one door, at the rear, a bit like the refrigerator where you might store the cheese. As a result, exiting could be interesting, or even impossible, in the case of a rear shunt.

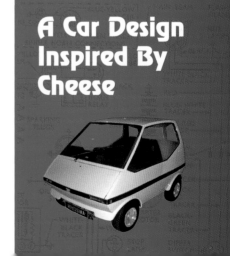

A Car Design Inspired By Cheese

Nissan Cedric & Gloria

- The Cedric and Gloria were the top models in the Nissan range for forty-four years, from 1960–2004.
- They were spacious, luxurious, comfortable, handled superbly, had sporty engines, were fast, accelerated like a Ferrari, and were good value and handsome.
- OK, that's all lies. They were outrageously expensive, handled like a jelly, had antique engines, performed like an asthmatic sloth, had seats which would look more at home in a pimp's boudoir, in profile looked a little like a Coke bottle, and depreciated so quickly that after two weeks of ownership you had to pay someone to take it off your hands.
- But they were quite reliable and made good minicabs in their later life.

The real reason they are here is their ludicrous names: Cedric is a middle-aged uncle figure wearing a cardigan and smoking a pipe; Gloria is a tarty middle-aged hooker standing on a street corner in Leeds touting for business. How could they expect to sell any expensive luxury saloons in the UK called Cedric or Gloria?

Apparently, Nissan wanted to give their cars more 'personality' by using people's names. The problem is they got it so dreadfully wrong. Do you really want to drive around in a Cedric? In a way, it is a pity the European car industry did not follow Nissan's example and launch the Lamborghini Hubert, Ferrari Frederick, Bugatti Basil, Jaguar Arthur, Land Rover Julian and Vauxhall Cynthia. It is said that the name Cedric was chosen by the then CEO of Nissan because that was the main character in the novel *Little Lord Fauntleroy*. Why he didn't simply call it the Nissan Lord Fauntleroy, we'll never know.

In fact, the whole story is complicated even more by the history of the two names. Originally, the Gloria was the top model of the Prince Car Company, which was taken over by Nissan. The Gloria was then positioned as the 'sporty' Cedric. Prince Gloria, and Gloria as a sporty Cedric? It all sounds a tad transgender to me.

Finally, in 2004 Nissan realised how silly these names were and introduced a new model. They gave it the sensible name of Fuga. Care is required in pronouncing that one.

BOND BUG

The Bond Bug was one of those ideas which at the time seemed different but not completely bizarre, and yet to modern eyes appears crazy. Today, if you suggested building a car which …

- was a sporty version of Del Boy's banger, with a similar propensity to topple over at the mention of the word 'corner'
- was capable of 78mph, so could topple over at considerable speed
- looked like a cross between a door wedge and a pack of Tesco's Red Leicester cheese
- had a single door like a clamshell, which on the basic model had to be propped open with a stay
- had no way of escape if you turned over
- was available in any colour so long as it was bright orange

- had the same 700cc engine as Del Boy, but which bizarrely shared the passenger compartment with the driver and passenger
- had no side windows, just flexible screens, and these were optional extras on the basic model
- at £629 cost more than a Mini, yet only had three wheels …

… you might risk being taken away in a padded van.

But in its day – in spite of its price – the Bond Bug was a moderate commercial success, with 2,268 being sold. These days it has a fanatical following, and quite reasonable survival rates. The bodywork was all plastic, the engine all aluminium, and the simple space frame well protected … so they'll probably last forever!

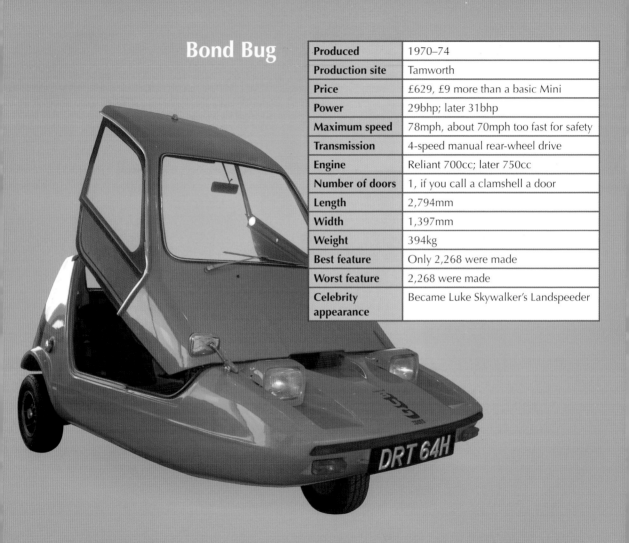

Bond Bug

Produced	1970–74
Production site	Tamworth
Price	£629, £9 more than a basic Mini
Power	29bhp; later 31bhp
Maximum speed	78mph, about 70mph too fast for safety
Transmission	4-speed manual rear-wheel drive
Engine	Reliant 700cc; later 750cc
Number of doors	1, if you call a clamshell a door
Length	2,794mm
Width	1,397mm
Weight	394kg
Best feature	Only 2,268 were made
Worst feature	2,268 were made
Celebrity appearance	Became Luke Skywalker's Landspeeder

DRT 64H

CHRYSLER AIRFLOW

The 1934 Chrysler Airflow is almost universally rated as one of the worst cars of all time. It merits inclusion here not so much because it was really bad, which it wasn't (well, actually it was), but because it must be the most ill-timed car in the history of motoring.

The simple fact is that in 1934 the American public was just not ready for a car that looked like a cross between a fireman's helmet and a jelly mould. If you gave a primary school pupil a potato and a knife and asked them to carve a car, chances are it would look rather like the

Airflow. Even though it did have a low drag coefficient, which must have worked in its favour, at the time most Americans would probably have thought a drag coefficient was some measure of how sleazy a speakeasy was.

Some people praise it as being the first car design which really understood aerodynamics. That's a bit like saying Noah developed the concept of the modern animal sanctuary, or that the Dead Sea Scrolls were the original design inspiration for the USB memory stick. There was also one slight technical

issue caused by the radical spaceframe construction. The engine had a habit of falling out. If you think that's serious, you might be accused of being a tad pernickety. Oh yes, and as its wheels were right in the corners, and the heavy engine was placed directly over the front axle to ensure the maximum amount of room for passengers, it wasn't very keen on hearing words like 'corner' or 'brake hard'.

Chrysler tried using publicity stunts to boost sales. In one, an Airflow was driven at 95.7mph through the flying mile at Bonneville Salt Flats (no corners, of course). In another, an Airflow was dropped off a 110ft cliff and then driven away. I suppose this at least demonstrated that the poor cornering ability need not be too much of a practical concern for those living in really hilly country. I think a better stunt might have been for the designer to jump off the top of the Empire State Building wearing nothing but a tiger skin jock strap.

Sales were abysmal … a bit like the styling really.

The Tropfenwagen was quite a good example of an ingenious design, but one which got nearly everything wrong for the contemporary car-buying market. Yet in some ways it was ninety years ahead of its time, which certainly qualifies it as 'bizarre'.

However, whether ahead of its time or not, the design included some slight drawbacks:

- Cooling for the engine was abysmal.
- Steering was abysmal.
- Power output was abysmal – 36bhp to move 3,000lb.
- Its appearance was abysmal, and its Cyclops 'eye' scared horses and children, and even left adults having bad dreams for days afterwards. Given the awful sales figures, not too many people actually had to look at one thankfully.
- There was no luggage compartment in spite of having room for six or seven passengers.
- Its name was far from inspirational: Rumpler was bad enough, but unavoidable; Tropfenwagen meant 'drop car'.

- It also shared a problem with a number of the other bizarre cars featured here: it was almost impossible from a distance to distinguish the front from the rear, and thereby tell what way it was about to move.

Believe it or not, the design gained the attention of Mercedes-Benz's chief engineer, Hans Nibel, who planned to design a racing version on the same chassis. Poor sales of the Tropfenwagen led to this idea being dropped. The Tropfenwagen only sold around 100, and two are known to survive.

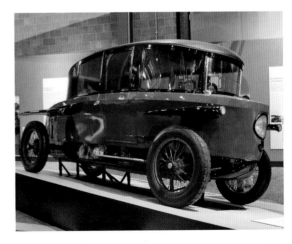

Rumpler Tropfenwagen

- The designer, Edward Rumpler, was born in Vienna and became an aircraft designer until he launched the Tropfenwagen.
- Thanks to its airship gondola shape it had a drag coefficient of just 0.28 when contemporary cars were around 0.60.
- Its engine was a W6 of 2,580cc.
- The W6 engine had three banks of paired cylinders driving one crankshaft.
- The layout was similar to that used in the latest Bentley W12 and Bugatti Veyron, although the Tropfenwagen's engine was virtually two-dimensional, being large but almost flat and just one cylinder in thickness.
- Power output was just 36bhp, or a miserable 14bhp per litre.
- The engine, gearbox, transmission and final drive were in a single bolt-on unit designed for easy repair.

The Mercedes G-Wagen may look like an ordinary jeep, a simple 4x4 perfect for farmers, rural voyeurs, pig sexers, mud fetishists – indeed anyone getting out into the great outdoors. We've all seen them in these great outdoors, doing the school run in Fulham, parked outside Waitrose, or collecting a load of DIY stuff from B&Q. Just the sort of places where mud-plugging 4x4 super torque, transfer boxes, lockable differentials, built-in winches and hill descent control are essential these days.

So why has it merited inclusion as a bizarre vehicle? There are several reasons:

1 It is quite unremittingly pig ugly.

2 It looks like the loser in a kindergarten origami competition.

3 In particular it resembles two milk crates stacked together.

4 It isn't even a Mercedes-Benz. It's actually a Steyr built in Austria.

5 All the panels are flat, and as we all know, flat panels dent whereas curved ones don't.

6 Its ability to climb 80-degree slopes and traverse 54-degree grades must be a real plus in isolated rural areas like Hampstead and Wimbledon, where it is most often seen.

7 Even the basic model costs about as much as twenty-five Range Rovers (OK, let's say twenty-four).

8 Best of all, when the designers were challenged on why it was so, well, square, their amazingly enlightening and totally bizarre answer was that it makes good use of the internal space, and makes it easier to drive down narrow rocky gullies.

On that last point, I would like to know how many Chelsea mums collecting Henry from the playgroup and Caroline from her ballet lesson suddenly encounter steep-sided rocky gullies in SW1. It's not as if we're talking about south of the river, for heaven's sake! And use of internal space? Bus shelters and portacabins are quite good at that, and better looking than the G-Wagen.

The G-Wagen must rate as one of the most unnecessary vehicles outside of the military. In twenty-five years of production the message still hasn't sunk in: it's grossly overpriced, it's less attractive than a breeze block, handles just marginally better, and is, quite simply, totally unnecessary. But most bizarrely of all, it was originally designed as a civilian vehicle, and only later moved to military applications when so few normal people bought one. You can still buy a new one if you are rich and stupid enough. You can even get one with a 600bhp V12 engine, which in practical terms must be on a par with strapping an enormous outboard motor to a floating turd.

The Bizarre World of Lifestyle Vehicles

Car manufacturers love 'lifestyle vehicles'. They are basically good for sales and revenues. Simply take a model which is already hopelessly out of date, such as the Jeep, with sales plummeting faster than a free-fall parachutist, saw a few bits off (especially the useful bits), stick some more on, give it a ludicrous name and hideous paint scheme, and there you have it … a new lifestyle vehicle … the Jeep Wrangler.

There is just one slight problem here. Real people's lifestyles are simply too mind-numbingly boring to be the subject of a new car. For example, what sort of exciting car could anyone design for these lifestyles:

> A middle-aged, overweight, insurance salesman called Brian who picks his nose and eats the snot, farts quite a lot, has a smelly dog called Colin and two awful teenage kids he can't stand, a wife called Doreen and no hobbies apart from darts, beer, picking fluff out of his navel and page 3 of *The Sun*.

> A 29-year-old bearded, ginger-haired techno nerd who wears socks with sandals, still lives at home with his parents, doesn't know what girls are, spends every evening in his bedroom playing computer games or surfing the net, has 1,575 'online good friends' but no real ones, and works part time in an abattoir whilst waiting for the 'big one' at Microsoft.

You see, real lives are simply not convenient for the car designer. So what they do instead is design the 'lifestyle' car first, then work out a new lifestyle to suit it. The fact that nobody on earth actually lives that lifestyle is an irrelevant detail.

We've already seen a number of lifestyle cars with non-existent lifestyles, including the Talbot Wind and Simca Matra Rancho. Nobody ever needed any of these cars because nobody led the mythical lifestyle they were designed for. Manufacturers also like 'lifestyle' categories in the car market. So we've now got CRV, SUV and MPV, 'soft-roader' and, of course, the 'Crossover', for when the manufacturers themselves can't even decide.

Mercedes G-Wagen

Maybach Facts

The Maybach is mainly bought by people who don't know much about cars but want other people to believe they do, and who are so ludicrously rich they can splash out the price of a decent Home Counties house on a car nobody has even heard of. In the unlikely event that any of these mega-rich people read this book, I have put the facts about the Maybach, in this case the 62S, in a form they will understand – or rather a form they won't understand but would like other people to think they do.

Engine capacity	8 bottles of Moët & Chandon, 1982
Number of seats	1 pleb up front, plus up to 4 rich Henries and high-class totties in the back
Price	16 x annual boarding fees at Eton
Maximum speed	4.8 x maximum speed of a Sunseeker 45 cruiser
0–60 time	The average delay between the indecent proposal and the facial slap at an après-ski party in Chamonix
Length	81 cans of 50g Beluga Caviar from Fortnums
Width	26 cans same
Weight	14 million diamond carats
Best feature	They've stopped making it
Worst feature	They waited eleven years too long to stop making it

Now we come to what must be the worst misunderstanding of the car-buying market's needs of the last four decades. This is the tale of the bizarre Maybach 57 & 62. After failing to buy either Rolls-Royce or Bentley, which went to BMW and Volkswagen respectively, Mercedes-Benz felt their nose had been put out of joint and decided to develop a rival ultra-luxury brand of their own.

So how did they go about this challenging task?

1. They chose the name Maybach, which means absolutely nothing to anyone unless you are German and aged over 90.

2. As the basis they took the chassis of the ageing S-Class, which had become so long in the tooth it was overdue for replacement.

3. They stretched this chassis until the whole car looked hideously out of proportion, rather like an S-Class viewed in a fairground mirror, and as a result the handling was totally compromised.

4. The styling was less exciting than that of an 8-year-old Ford Mondeo, a common result of trying too hard, in the same way Lexus had done with the LS400.

5. They used the same engine as for the S-Class, but bolted on massive turbos to give it enough power to move the car's 3 tons, in the process losing all the engine's natural smooth charm.

6. They insisted that motoring journalists didn't drive the cars themselves, but were 'chauffeured' for road tests because 'that's how most Maybachs would be driven'.

7. They never marketed the car to owner/drivers, maybe because the dynamics and handling were so dreadful that such an experience was best left to a paid chauffeur.

8. They built the Maybach on the same production line as the S-Class, with no differentiation to make it appear super luxury.

9. They priced the Maybach at four times the price of the S-Class. The top-of-the-range model was priced at not far short of $1 million, about ten times that of a relatively similar S-Class Merc.

10. They appointed Ulrich Schmid-Maybach as the 'brand ambassador' for the car, even though nobody had ever heard of him and he may not even have existed – and nobody knew what a brand ambassador was anyway.

11 They tried to make the interior super luxury, which for a German car maker meant they made the wood even more like plastic, and the leather even more like vinyl. (Germans just cannot do super-luxury interiors, just as the French can't do large cars.)

12 To justify the outrageous price tag, they thought up totally unnecessary features, like a voice-activated sunroof, heated cup holders and a 21-speaker sound system. How do you even find twenty-one different places in a car to put a speaker?

They assumed they'd sell over 2,000 each year, but global sales never exceeded 250 per annum, and by 2010 only sixty-three gullible people worldwide could be found to have bought one. Unfortunately for them, public awareness of the Maybach was so dismally low that few, if any, people would have realised how much they had spent.

Not surprisingly, with sales running at just 3% of those planned, the plug was pulled. It is most unusual for a car's sales to fall every single year after launch, but with the Maybach, Mercedes-Benz managed to achieve the impossible.

TALBOT TAGORA

Although the Tagora was produced as recently as 1983, I can guarantee you'll not find a single person who's ever heard of it unless they're wearing a 'Chrysler Europe Rocks!!' t-shirt. And even then they might be too embarrassed to admit knowledge of this automotive lemon. It looks harmless enough, so what went wrong?

I feel it's another example from a car designer with no friends, who never goes out, wears socks with sandals, and thinks the car-buying public is some little-understood malevolent alien species featuring in their latest computer game. So let's examine the issues:

- Chrysler Europe decided to market it under the Talbot name. Unfortunately, the only people who have actually heard of the Talbot name in Britain are a small group of 78-year-old, cravat-wearing, real ale enthusiasts who live in Epsom and fondly remember the 1948 Talbot Lago (which was a great car).
- It was meant to be an upmarket executive car. However, it was designed and built in France, and, as we know, the French simply cannot do big cars.
- In a sector where smooth 3-litre, 6-cylinder engines are the norm, Chrysler decided to use instead a crude 2.2-litre four-pot job. Why they didn't go the whole hog and fit a rough diesel tractor engine, I'll never know.
- The style was succinctly summed up by *What Car?* magazine as follows: 'The Tagora has such a complete blandness of style as to disqualify it instantly in a market where character and status count for so much.' Praise indeed.
- There was a problem finding the right rear axle for the Tagora, and they made do with one from the much narrower Peugeot 505, resulting in a truly bizarre crab-like appearance. The plan had been to conceal this design 'feature' (car designers always call design faults 'features') behind spats, which is one of the few things I can think of which would have made an abysmal car even worse.
- A steeply angled windscreen and a short wedge-shaped bonnet gave the car a look customers were not accustomed to; in the automotive design world the technical term for this would be 'pig ugly'.

Tagora was mercifully 'put to sleep' in 1983 after just three years. Symptomatic of the health of Chrysler Europe at the time the Tagora was being developed is the fact that the American parent company sold the business to the French PSA Group for a massively over-valued $1. They didn't get a bargain.

Talbot Tagora

- It was a 'big' car but designed in France, which was of course a recipe for failure.
- It was only produced for four years, 1980–83, but even that was four years too long.
- Three engines were available: a 2.2-litre petrol which was a reheated Simca 180 unit; a 2.3-litre turbo diesel which delivered a pathetic 80bhp; and a 2.7-litre V6 petrol.
- Uniquely for a major car manufacturer, an automatic was available on the 'base' models but not on the expensive 'range topping' V6.
- Only 1,083 of the V6s were ever sold.
- Sales never exceeded 10% of plan.
- By 2010, 99.09% of all Tagoras in Britain had disappeared from the road.

AMC PACER

The Pacer was manufactured by AMC between 1975 and 1980. In terms of the US market it can only rate as slightly bizarre, on the modest grounds that:

1   It looked like a cross between a jellybean and a particularly hideous fish tank mounted on a skateboard.

2   About half its external bodywork was glass.

3   Although classed as a compact car, it maintained the width of a full-size American, at an amazing 6ft 6in. Given that the car was only 14ft long, it was probably the most 'square' normal car ever made.

4   The car was originally designed to take a Wankel engine, but a change of mind left the Pacer without an engine at all, and it was announced to the public in this engine-less state.

5   The door on the passenger side was 4in longer than the one on the driver's side.

This latter point was not a simple draughtsman's error on a Friday afternoon. Well, it might have been, but the marketing guys devised a great wheeze to conceal this oversight. They claimed the idea was to make it easier for passengers to get into the back seats from the nearside pavement, whilst keeping the driver's door smaller for safety when opening it towards the traffic.

OK, so in the US market it was rather quirky. However, it became really bizarre when imported into the UK. This was because:

a It was only produced in left-hand drive and the UK importer didn't bother to switch around the steering column; instead he installed a chain drive across the car to work the steering from a wheel on the right side – technology you might expect to find on a nineteenth-century ship.

b The asymmetric doors meant that in the UK passengers had to squeeze through the small 'driver's' door to get into the back, whilst the driver swung open his outsized door into the flow of traffic, possibly blocking a couple of lanes in the process.

c When stocked with just a few extras, the Pacer weighed in at a massive 1.5 tons – not what the Brits would call a 'compact' – and fuel consumption was somewhere amongst the upper reaches of prodigious.

d Being wider than a Rolls-Royce Silver Shadow, this 'compact' car had certain access problems.

e In addition, it was not available in the UK with any engine smaller than a 3.8-litre 6.

AMC believed they were thinking 'outside the box' when it came to the Pacer's design. I think the designers should have been kept inside the box, and maybe the key thrown away.

The terms '3 litre' and 'Westminster' have been applied to many Austin cars, from early post-war up until the 1970s, so in order to identify the 'bizarre' Austin we must be quite precise about the dates. Here I refer very specifically to the Austin 3 litre, introduced in 1968 and withdrawn as early as 1969 in standard form, and 1971 in deluxe form, after just 10,000 had been produced.

Austin 1800: the passenger compartment is identical to that on the new 'luxury' 3 litre.

I've always rather liked the Austin 3 litre. It was quite good-looking, luxurious and had a decent turn of speed. So why is it bizarre? We need to look back in time to answer this.

BMC, as it then was, followed up the highly successful Mini and Austin 1100 range with a new vehicle codenamed ADO17, which became known as the Austin/Morris/Wolseley 1800. It shared many features with the earlier successful models, including front-wheel drive, transverse engines, hydrolastic suspension, and a surprising amount of passenger space for the overall size of vehicle. It wasn't a bad car at all, although it did acquire the nickname 'land crab' on account of its long wheelbase and fairly square proportions.

So when BMC decided to launch a replacement for their previous top of the range Austin Westminster, did they build on the Mini/1100/1800 success story and introduce a new front-wheel drive, transverse engine, hydrolastically suspended, upmarket large saloon with inspiring new bodywork designed by a top Italian design house? Not quite. Rather than design a new bodyshell, they simply took the 1800 chassis and welded a longer bonnet and boot section to it.

It was decided that the engine for the new car would not be some super new transverse unit as in the 1800, but the old straight 6 3 litre used in the previous Westminster, and designed somewhere around the time of the Wars of the Roses. Due to its size it couldn't be formatted for front-wheel drive, so it drove the rear wheels like the old Westminster. Basically, they took the 1800 and threw away all the good bits, apart from the hydrolastic suspension. Given that the middle bit of the chassis was identical to the 1800, it didn't even have more passenger space – it had less, in fact, because of the large transmission tunnel.

The government loved it as a vehicle for whisking senior civil servants and ministers around. The public loathed it and sales were a disaster. Sir Alec Issigonis, who designed the Mini and 1100, was always keen to point out he had nothing to do with the 3 litre.

- The Maserati TC was a truly bizarre offering by any standards.

- It was marketed as the 'Chrysler TC by Maserati', which sounds more like a perfume or a pair of jeans. This suggests that even the manufacturer was embarrassed by it.

- The idea behind the TC was apparently 'to incorporate Chrysler's design and production concepts with those of Maserati, while keeping quality high and the price relatively low'.

- It was, in many ways, a truly international car. The chassis components, engine, and sheet steel for the body were shipped to Italy from the US. The wiring came from Spain, and other bits from both France and Germany. The whole lot was assembled at Maserati's Innocenti plant near Milan and then shipped to the States.

- Although the idea of building a super-sexy body in Italy and installing reliable high-tech mechanicals inside may be basically sound, unfortunately there were two flaws in the plot: firstly, the car didn't look at all exotic, but virtually identical to the US-made Chrysler LeBaron, which cost $13,500 less; secondly, the engines were dull – either exactly the same Mitsubishi V6 as in the LeBaron, or, even

worse, a 2.2-litre four pot married to a 3-speed automatic which struggled to get the 1,375kg TC to 60mph in less than 11 seconds.

- So rather than an exotic Italian supercar at a reasonable price, buyers got an overpriced LeBaron which had travelled halfway round the world to acquire its all-pervading dullness.

- Problems continued in the interior, which had strangely ruched leather; it would have looked more at home in a typical blingy pimpmobile.

- The fit and finish were poor by any standards. And it shared a few components with the LeBaron: door handles, door locks, window switches, parking brake, gauges, turn signal stalks, steering column, dash vents, ashtray, glove box, cassette holder, climate control, stereo, windscreen … the list goes on. But it did sport a Maserati badge, which by my reckoning cost around $10,000.

The plan had been to sell 5,000 per year through carefully selected dealers. However, after three years the total sold was 7,300. The TC fell into the same trap as the Alfa Romeo Arna – put an exotic badge on mind-numbingly boring crap and all you end up with is mind-numbingly boring crap with an exotic badge on it. The public don't buy that, metaphorically and literally.

Oh, and what did TC stand for? I don't know, but Total Crap would have been quite appropriate.

The United States has produced its fair share of muscle cars, ones that breathe fire and eat normal cars for breakfast, spitting their remains out like pips. These have included the Ford Mustang, Dodge Charger, Pontiac Firebird and Chevrolet Camaro, all competing to be the bad boy on the block. When Chevrolet decided to launch a new version of the Camaro in 1982, the Iron Duke, it was expected that this bully would finally nail the Mustang to the floor and rub its nose in its own excrement. It certainly looked the part, but it didn't quite work out like that.

Rather than a bully, Chevrolet produced something more akin to the skinny, spotty kid in glasses who hides under his desk at school to avoid the big boys. For this new Camaro they chose a limp-wristed, 2.5-litre, straight 4 allied to an antiquated 3-speed 'slush box'. There was a time when its 85bhp might have set the world alight, but that time was somewhere around 1919.

This puny lump struggled to get the heavy Iron Duke to 60mph in under 20 seconds. There was a rumour that the drivers of refuse collection trucks and school buses in the US petitioned to get the Iron Dukes banned from the roads during daylight hours as they delayed their progress too much. In some states combine harvester drivers would show off by out-dragging an Iron Duke away from the traffic lights.

Another slight technical problem with the Iron Duke engine was that after about 80,000 miles, it had a rather annoying habit of simply falling to pieces. I suppose that could be seen in a positive light if it helped remove these motorised disasters from the roads.

There was, however, a sliver of silver lining to what was otherwise an enormous grey cloud. Buy an Iron Duke rather than a Camaro with a more appropriate 7-litre V8 and at least you'd be safe from speeding tickets.

Bizarre Ways to Market a Premium Brand: Part 2

Bizarre Car Names: Part 4

And so the creativity of the marketing guys goes on …

Geely Rural Nanny & Urban Nanny	There's not much to add about these two.
Volkswagen Thing	Yes, Volkswagen in their wisdom really did call their jeep-type thing a Thing! In some markets it was also known as the Type 181. The creative guys must have scratched their heads for days trying to think up a new name. Then presumably the boss walked in and asked, 'Have you decided what to call that thing yet?' … and bingo!
AMC Gremlin	This speaks for itself.
Vauxhall Nova	In Spanish *nova* means 'doesn't go'.
Dodge Swinger	This definitely conjures up exciting thoughts about a simple road journey.
Volkswagen Bora	In Iceland *bora* means 'rectum'.
Seat Ronda	In Hungarian *ronda* means 'ugly', but appropriately the car is also hideous.
SsangYong Musso	In Arabic *musso* means 'suck him'.
Citroen Xsara Picasso	In Portuguese *picasso* means a 'really large penis'.

OK, it's not really called the Flintstone, it's the Plymouth Prowler, produced from 1997–2002. But it bore an uncanny resemblance to the car driven by Fred Flintstone, except that Flintstone's vehicle was marginally more attractive and sensible. From certain angles, the Prowler resembled a cross between some sort of kitchen appliance and a log splitter.

Plymouth Prowler is hardly an inspiring name, and sounds like a dodgy character in a dirty raincoat. I wonder if they had considered the Plymouth Stalker instead? The design is said to have derived from Chrysler's engineers being given a free hand to create 'whatever they wanted in a hot rod or sportster type vehicle'. I suppose a simple lesson was learned from this – don't give engineers a free hand.

The engineers were clearly so preoccupied with the hot rod or sportster bit that they forgot the car would be bought by real people. Part of their 'free hand' forgot to include anything which might loosely be described as a boot (or trunk, as it was an American car). So dire was the complete lack of luggage storage that, amazingly, one really bizarre optional extra was a trailer to tow behind the Prowler which would hold your bags. The trailer was designed to look like a second rear end. Call me a traditionalist, but towing a trailer does tend to detract just a tad from the sporty image of any two-seat sports car, and kill any semblance of 'cool'. They could have called the car Two Bums (or Two Butts, as it was American).

In their enthusiasm the designers also forgot that the car would need a front number plate. The photograph shows a number plate rather self-consciously pop-riveted to one of the front 'bumpers'. At high speed this must have acted rather like an aileron, causing the car to veer sharply to the left.

At least they gave the Prowler a half-decent motor, a 3.5-litre V6 SOHC, producing 214bhp and giving a 0–60 time of around 7 seconds and a top speed of 118mph; so at least you could quickly escape the derision of pedestrians. Of course, the slight downside was that when towing the essential trailer, speed was limited by law to 55mph.

FIAT MULTIPLA

The Fiat Multipla was actually quite a good vehicle and won a lot of acclaim, especially on account of its flexible interior design. It was *Top Gear* Car of the Year in 2000 and was voted *Top Gear* magazine's Family Car of the Year for four years in a row (2001–04). Its claim for bizarreness lies with one small design 'feature', which as we know is the car manufacturer's euphemism for 'fault'.

It is clear that the Multipla was designed by two separate teams which never met, one working from the ground up to waist level, and the other working from the roofline down to the waist. The problem was that the first team thought they were designing a conventional car with a bonnet, whilst the second team were convinced it was to be more like a minibus. When the two halves of the design were finally brought together, they simply did not match up. It became evident that both teams had thought they were doing the headlights. Plus the location of the Fiat badge is as it would be on a minibus!

Obviously neither team would back down and admit their mistake, so the Multipla was launched with its split personality. No doubt it appealed to buyers where, for example, the husband wanted a normal car and the wife preferred something more bus-like, but these buyers were thin on the ground and outside Italy sales were very poor indeed. Eventually, a saner version was launched after the two design teams met up and started talking, and sales picked up.

The lesson to be learned here is that members of the public like to buy a car which has been designed as one car, not two.

Two-Wheeled Bizarreness

NER-A-CAR

The name Ner-a-Car was supposed to be a clever play on words. The vehicle was created by a certain Carl A. Neracher, and was built in Syracuse, USA, and in Sheffield, England, by the Sheffield Simplex Company. It was aimed at people who couldn't afford a car but wanted something more like a car than a motorcycle. It had two interesting technical details: an infinitely variable transmission and a centre hub steering system.

Now, what confuses me a little is why it is 'ner' to a car. It's not a car; it's a bleeding motorcycle, and a stupid-looking one at that. If that is 'ner' a car then my bathtub is 'ner' an Olympic swimming pool. And whilst we're talking about comparisons to a car, it only carried one person, there was no weather protection, and it made the 'driver' look like a complete prat. Also, the centre hub steering was prone to making it topple over. So much for it being 'ner a car'.

And why did the company fail in the end? It tried to introduce an expensive luxury model. Come on, for heaven's sake, all your customers have gone and bought a proper car! I think Carl A. Neracher missed an opportunity to build up a big brand here. Put a wicker basket on the back

and we'd have the Ner-a-Juggernaut. Install a second seat and we get the Ner-a-Routemaster. Tie a spade to the front … the Ner-a-JCB. The possibilities are ner-endless.

Sixty years ago Royal Enfield launched the Bullet, and one variant was diesel powered. It enjoyed brief popularity on account of its prodigious fuel economy, even though it could be overtaken by a geriatric one-legged hedgehog using a Zimmer frame. Did it die away completely? No. They are still making it in India. Having said that, it is slightly younger than the Hindustan Ambassador, which is actually the 1948 Morris Oxford.

The standard model has a 350cc engine, but the 'deluxe' model in the photograph carries the much more sporty 436cc engine, which churns out an earth-moving 7.5bhp. This is enough, it is believed, to propel it up to 55mph. Why believed? Well, although it can do 200 miles to the gallon and, with a 3.8-gallon tank, enjoy a range of 760 miles, that is still not a long enough distance to get above 52mph, so it would be necessary to stop for fuel on the way up to 55mph. Oh, and you need to use all five gears to reach 30mph.

There are two useful features of the bike: it will happily run on cooking oil, which takes the diesel cost equivalent mpg to 500 miles (rumours it will run on softened

A late 1950s model of the Royal Enfield Bullet.

A diesel Triumph Speed Triple ... a Bullet with 'grunt'.

tarmac mixed with nail varnish and Dulux gloss white are thought to be exaggerated); and when under any load – which in essence means any time it is actually moving – it expels great clouds of black noxious, carcinogenic fumes from the rear, perfect for forcing that annoying vehicle tailgating you to quickly back off. Five hundred miles to the gallon? It would make good sense to befriend the local MacDonald's manager for his used chip fat.

Incidentally, I understand it is the slowest vehicle road-tested in any magazine or newspaper over the last twenty years. It was possible to run over a plant with the front wheel, only for the plant to recover and flower again before being flattened by the rear wheel. That was how slow it was. The road tester used a calendar rather than a stopwatch to obtain the acceleration times. It might have benefited from some sails to take advantage of any following wind.

However, the story does not end with the Bullet. A popular conversion is to create a diesel Triumph Speed Triple by transplanting an industrial 3-cylinder diesel unit into a Speed Triple frame. It may look like a cross between a garden rotavator and a cement mixer, but this does seem to resolve the issue about performance with the Bullet.

At first glance, the Münch Mammut looks like a fairly normal motorcycle, albeit quite a big one. But if you look more closely you'll see a difference. The engine is as wide as a car engine. There is a good reason for this – it *is* a car engine.

People are familiar with the many cars powered by motorcycle engines, such as the early Morgans. But Herr Friedel Münch wondered why it all had to be one-way traffic from bike to car; why not do the reverse? And that is what he did.

Herr Friedel Münch, otherwise known as the Sorcerer of Ossenheim, had decided that all existing bike engines were, well, a little limp and wet. He decided instead to install the air-cooled, four-stroke, 4-cylinder, 1,289cc overhead cam engine from the NSU Prinz. Great concept, the only downside being that the engine was so wide the rider had to sit well behind it. The whole bike weighed 630lb, of which around 629.8lb was the engine.

Münch being Münch, by 1978 he had decided his existing range was just too tame and probably better suited to hairdressers or middle-aged vicars' wives than 'real' bikers. So he upped the spec to a 1,400cc NSU car engine with fuel injection and a turbocharger. This increased the power from a 'girlie' 88bhp of the earlier bikes to a hairy-chested 143bhp, or well over 500bhp/ton.

It was a pity the words 'disc brake' were not in Mr Münch's Ladybird Book of How to Build Hideously Fast Bikes, so stopping could be entertaining, in spite of the largest drum brakes ever fitted to two wheels. Although no longer made, the Mammut did spawn a whole series of monstrous car-engined bikes, including ones powered by a Rover V8 and even a supercharged Chevrolet V8.

Two-wheeled bizarreness: the Münch Mammut, a car between your knees. (Courtesy of Andrew Breedon)

MTT STREETFIGHTER

On the face of it, the MTT Streetfighter looks like a normal sporty motorcycle, but it does have a bizarre secret. The giveaway is the rather larger-than-normal exhaust pipe.

The Streetfighter is powered not by some weedy, limp-wristed, 10,000cc, 48-cylinder piston engine running on pure vodka and space dust. No, it is actually powered by the gas turbine engine from a helicopter. So basically, it's just a normal motorcycle with a bit more power which makes a screaming noise. To show how similar it is to the sort of ordinary bike we are familiar with, the fact box shows a

comparison between the Streetfighter and the 1971 BSA Bantam, the last year of production of this iconic British machine. As they are so similar the two bikes have been labelled A and B, and you need to tell which is which. It could be hard so take your time.

MTT Streetfighter vs BSA Bantam

One of the two bikes is the Streetfighter. See if you can work out which one.

	A	B
Produced	2000–present	1948–71
Number made	Few	400,000
Price	$175,000	£150
Power	420bhp	4.5bhp
Maximum speed	227mph	45mph
Rpm	52,000*	5,000
Bhp/ton	1,882	56
Tank capacity	34 litres	8 litres
Mpg	~3	80
Weight	500lb	180lb
Range	~22 miles	142 miles

Note: Power up to 51,999rpm = ~1bhp. Power at 52,000rpm and above = 420bhp.

There is one slight snag to this splendid bizarre vehicle. It runs, of course, on aviation fuel and so can only fill up at airfields. With a tank of only 34 litres, and prodigious fuel consumption, journeys have to be planned carefully from airfield to airfield. Actually, that is a lie, as it can run on diesel as well, but the airfield bit makes a better story.

Another slight snag is the exhaust. The exhaust blast from the turbine is liable to reduce nearby pedestrians' legs to barbequed satay sticks. Given that the bike is made in the US, where they drive on the wrong side of the road, the decision to place the exhaust on the *right* side of the bike might suggest a small degree of sadism by the designers. It may or may not be true that you can tell where a Streetfighter has been ridden from the barbequed pedestrians left in its wake.

The V8 iron block engine has become virtually synonymous with Motown, but Detroit's very first V8 back in 1913 was not a car. Instead it was a really bizarre two-wheeled creation called the Scripps Booth Bi-Autogo. The fact that it sounds like 'bye, ought to go' was perhaps slightly prophetic.

Although it was the size and weight of a car, it had only two wheels so technically was a motorcycle. It also had two outrigger wheels like a kid's bike, or even the Schilovski Gyrocar. These were raised above 20mph, at which speed the gyroscopic effect of the heavy wheels, allied to a good chunk of faith, would help keep it balanced. Its massive 6.3-litre V8 engine produced just 45bhp, or a miserable 7bhp per litre – less than one-tenth of the typical later V8. Bizarrely, it was started by compressed air stored in two tanks pressurised from an engine-mounted compressor and it was steered by a car-like steering wheel. A 'feature' of the steering was that when the wheel was turned to change direction, the front of the massive vehicle was lowered by up to 0.5in, so on returning to the straight ahead position the 'driver' effectively had to raise the 1.5-ton lump whilst turning the steering wheel.

It carried three passengers in tandem and it had wooden wheels, which must have inspired great confidence. It weighed a staggering 1,451kg, so the outriggers were essential because, should the machine topple sideways, no rider would be able to right it again. It also had a massive, bizarre, copper tube radiator like an enormous pair of gills extending down both sides, so it looked more like a mobile distillery than a motorcycle.

It was fortunate for the designer that he was the heir to a huge publishing empire, so he could indulge his whims. The Scripps Booth Company was eventually bought by General Motors, having moved on from the Bi-Autogo to more normal cars.

The Megola is bizarre because it was a front-wheel drive motorcycle. By looking at it, the feature which probably stands out the most is that it appears to have no engine. The bit in front of the rider, which would normally accommodate the odd cylinder or two, looks to be totally empty. Was this an unfortunate oversight on the part of the designers?

Maybe it was only designed for going downhill and didn't actually need an engine? No. The truth is that it had an engine but it was inside the front wheel. To add to the bizarreness rating, it was a rotary engine where the whole thing rotated and the crankshaft was fixed. It wasn't a small engine, either; it had 5 cylinders, 640cc, and developed so much

torque it needed neither clutch nor gears. Its power output wasn't quite so mind-boggling, however: a meagre 14bhp. But it could achieve around 52mph.

The name Megola was, apparently, intended to be a portmanteau word derived from the designers' names – <u>Me</u>ixner, <u>Co</u>ckerell and <u>La</u>ndgaf. But evidently someone was dyslexic as it should have been called the Mecola. Further indication of some degree of mental limitation was the decision to put the engine inside the front wheel, with all the implied complications, rather than the rear wheel, which would have avoided all the complexity. Maybe they were Megola-maniacs. It is fortunate the bike couldn't exceed 52mph as I suspect the gyroscopic precession upon turning a corner at any greater speed would have caused it to flip over, a problem which afflicted the Schilovski Gyrocar.

The Megola was produced from 1921 to 1925, and around 2,000 were built. After the war the baton for motorcycle bizarreness was clearly handed to the American

company Rokon, who started in the 1960s to produce two-wheel drive motorcycles (2x2) noted for their extreme slowness. They were designed to travel as slowly as 0.2mph over rough terrain, with a maximum of around 20mph. This glacial slowness was the result of an extreme lack of capacity and power (134cc and 6bhp) and the fact that two-wheel drive requires such a complicated combination of belts, chains, drive shafts, gear boxes, ropes and pulleys that most of the modest 6bhp produced got absorbed by the transmission before the remnants of the power reached the road. However, in spite of the complexity and almost total absence of performance they were popular with those who liked the 'great outdoors' … which helps if it's going to take you 5 hours to cover just 1 mile.

The Megola is Reborn!

In 1935 a group of German engineers tried to improve on the Megola and built the Killinger & Freund. The development of this was stopped by the war, which is probably not a bad thing as its appearance was scary. The only known photograph is the one shown here, in which an American GI is trying to work out exactly what the contraption is, as it looks like a pair of ice lollies mating, or maybe an outsized tin opener.

This reincarnation of the Megola has to go down as not just bizarre, but probably the ugliest thing ever to be carried on two wheels.

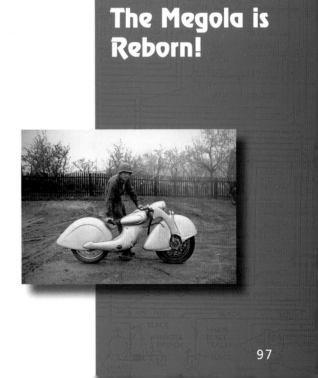

As a final brief excursion into the world of two-wheeled bizarreness, we come to the Hubbard Steamcycle. Steam cars, such as the Stanley and the White, were around from the earliest days of motoring, and were excellent vehicles in their own way. We have seen a diesel-powered motorcycle which set new standards for slowness. Now we encounter the steam motorbike.

The Hubbard was built by Arthur 'Bud' Hubbard in the 1970s ... actually most of the 1970s as it took him an age to build it from untested designs in *The Model Engineer* and *Electrician* magazine. It featured a 2-cylinder, 100cc, single-acting steam engine and it would run for up to 2 hours on a water fill-up, and used 1 gallon of petrol per hour. Rather like an aeroplane, fuel consumption was quoted in time not miles, as the steam had to be kept at full pressure even when stationary.

I can think of just a few concerns about steam motorcycles:

- Whenever you wanted to go somewhere, you'd have to wait whilst it got up steam.
- If you were, say, popping into the shops, you'd have to leave it steamed up outside.
- Some riders might be slightly concerned about having a boiler containing superheated steam between their legs.
- You'd ride along in billows of steam – quite pleasant in some ways, but not so great for the cars behind.

The steam motorcycle does have one great advantage over a normal petrol-engined one – it can make a lovely cup of tea!

A way for bikers to let off steam – the Hubbard Motorcycle. (Courtesy of James Anderson)

Sir Charles Dennistoun Burney Bt

Sir Charles Dennistoun Burney, the son of former Admiral of the Fleet Sir Cecil Burney Bt, born in 1888, may at first seem an unlikely character to have built such a bizarre car as the Streamline. He was managing director of the private firm which built the R100 airship (the one that didn't crash in flames in northern France) and he invented the 'paravane' as a device for cutting the cables holding mines under the sea. Later, together with Neville Shute (who became the famous author) he invented an air-launched gliding torpedo, and the first British recoilless rifle, known as the Burney Gun. He was also a Member of Parliament from 1922 to 1929. So what made him design such a bizarre car?

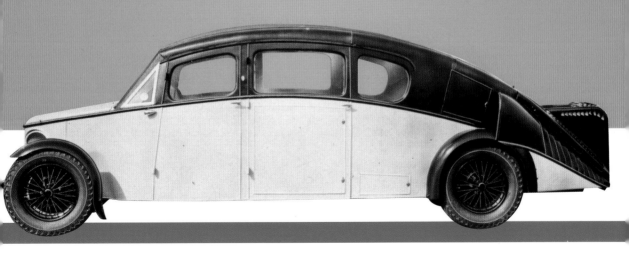

BURNEY STREAMLINE

Following his distinguished earlier career, when Charles Dennistoun Burney got a little older and presumably a little bored with sensible things like airships and torpedoes, he decided to turn his attention to road transport. I think one morning, after maybe a heavy night on the Beaujolais, he fell out of bed, banged his head, and came up with his brilliant idea. Why must cars look like cars, when with a little imagination and team work they could instead look like a cross between a dung beetle and an allotment tool shed with a cement mixer welded to the back and mounted on bicycle wheels? And so he came up with the Burney Streamline. What a brilliant piece of inspired design!

And since he thought that the appearance alone wasn't amusing enough, he mounted the spare wheel inside one of the rear doors, so it weighed about half a ton and could take your arm off. In addition, he made the cooling so abysmal it was like a greenhouse (albeit half as attractive) and he made the mobile potting shed nearly as expensive as a Rolls-Royce, and about 25ft long, so you couldn't park it anywhere. I suppose part of the joke was trying to work out which was the front end and which was the back.

The only saving grace was that he endowed his potting shed with a powerful twin cam, 4-litre Beverly Barnes engine which gave the car a decent turn of speed. As a result, embarrassed owners could at least get away quickly before anybody recognised them. This was an enormous engine, originally designed for aero use, which explains the protuberance at the back.

Between 1929 and 1933 he made twelve of these Streamlines, all different, although I don't know if that is a blessing or not. He even gave one to the Prince of Wales ... well, he had to give it; no one in their right mind would actually buy one!

He apparently tried to interest Bentley and Rolls-Royce into making these automotive failures, and I understand the laughter this provoked still echoes around the corridors there to this very day. When BMW and VW took over the two firms, it is said even the Germans found it funny and continued laughing.

In the end, Burney managed to persuade the Crosley company to make some. I can only assume the agreement was signed after an excessively boozy dinner. They tried to improve the look by welding a second cement mixer on the front and hiding it under some sort of false bonnet. At least now you could tell which way they were travelling. They made twenty-five of these before the embarrassment got too much.

Lessons to be learned by car manufacturers:

- potting sheds belong on allotments
- cement mixers belong on building sites
- bicycle wheels belong on bicycles
- spare wheels belong anywhere except inside doors

Poor old Sir Dennistoun belonged anywhere except near a car factory.

I believe one of the more 'sensible' Crosley cars survives, which sounds like a more than satisfactory survival rate to me.

The Only Car Designed by a Catholic Priest

The Aurora is, as far as I am aware, the only car ever designed by a Catholic priest. Father Alfred Juliano designed and started making the Aurora between 1957 and 1958, partially funded by his own parishioners. It was to be built on a Buick chassis with Chrysler, Cadillac or Lincoln engines. Unfortunately, it was a tad short of divine inspiration.

Father Juliano's intentions in building it were good, as you'd expect from a priest. He presumably didn't want too many of his parishioners going to meet their maker prematurely, so he set out to build the most pedestrian-safe car in history. Hence all the bulbous swoopy bodywork, particularly the front scoop, designed, I suppose, to gently pick up the unfortunate who has just been knocked down, and cushion and caress him in a sea of squidgy plastic bodywork until he can be gently and safely deposited on some soft grassy verge.

The car had many other safety features, novel at the time, but now routine. These features included seatbelts, a roll cage, side-impact bars, a collapsible steering column, a padded instrument panel, a confession box … oh, sorry, that was an optional extra. The most innovative safety feature, which fortunately has not been incorporated into other cars, was the ability to quickly swivel the seats to face rearwards should a collision seem imminent. That could be rather challenging to explain to the traffic police, I feel. It puts a new perspective on the claim 'I didn't see him, officer'.

The main problem was that, in designing a car with all these features, Juliano produced what is almost universally considered to be the ugliest wheeled vehicle ever to set tyre on Earth. Here is a summary of the main problems of the Aurora:

1   It was so hideously ugly no sane person would have bought one voluntarily, unless God offered help with marketing, or the car came with a 'free pass' through the Pearly Gates.

2   If they had wanted to buy one, they would have had to pay around $12,000, just $1,000 less than the most costly car in the US at the time, the Cadillac Eldorado Brougham. (OK, so the Cadillac wasn't that much better looking and handled like shit.)

3   The pedestrian safety aspects might have been overstated. I suspect most innocent pedestrians would have died of sheer fright at the sight of the Aurora approaching long before they impacted the car itself.

4   It was non-too reliable. The prototype broke down fifteen times on its way to the press launch in 1957 and had to be towed to seven different garages en route. I presume at the first six garages the mechanics were left helpless in uncontrollable fits of laughter. As a result, the total production run was significantly less than two.

Amazingly, the entire production run of one survives to this day, giving it probably the highest survival rate of any car made. It was found behind a garage in the US where, I presume, the last owner had left it, having been too embarrassed to have it on public display.

I suppose the key lesson from the Aurora is that Catholic priests should stick to what they do best: priesting and saving souls rather than pedestrians.

DYMAXION

This one is a first-rate candidate for the weirdest of all cars. The Dymaxion was designed by Buckminster Fuller in 1933. The 'car' had three wheels, with the single wheel being at the rear. It was able to turn around within its own length, although given its shape and height we might hope this was only performed at low speed. With the single steering wheel at the back, handling in tight corners, especially in cross winds, was said to be 'entertaining'. Using an aluminium body crafted on airplane principles, it weighed just 1,600lb, about the same as a VW Beetle, in spite of being over 20ft long and over 6ft high. It was designed to carry a driver and ten passengers. With a bhp Ford V8 engine, it was claimed to be capable of over 120mph, yet return over 30mpg. In reality, the top speed was more like 90mph and the world is probably safer for that. The front axle was also a Ford unit, but in this instance the rear axle of a Ford car turned around to provide front-wheel drive.

On paper that sounds impressive. But when you consider it had rear-wheel steering through its single rear wheel and was about as robust as a cigar tube (which it looked uncannily like), it would have taken a very brave or completely daft driver to try to reach 90mph. Indeed, the first prototype crashed at the 1933 Chicago World Fair killing the driver and seriously injuring two passengers. And if that wasn't enough, it was designed, believe it or not, to travel not only on land and water, but also in the air, upon attachment of suitable wings. Well, if you thought driving a rear-steer cigar tube holding eleven people at 120mph on a road was a little too sober, sensible and safe, then surely landing your Dymaxion at Heathrow between jumbo jets will have tickled your fancy. In a later version Fuller mounted the single, steering rear wheel out on a long boom. It then looked a little like a sausage on the end of a cocktail stick.

The Dymaxion was not a raging success. I can't think why. Just three were made, and at least one survives. Maybe the Dymaxion was just a little too conservative and ordinary for an American public which had radical ideas, like, for example, that a car should look just a tad like a car. Buckminster Fuller also tried building houses the same way. Is it any surprise his car was one wheel short of a full chassis? Maybe overall Buckminster Fuller was ahead of his time, although we are still left wondering what that time was, and whether it will ever arrive.

Richard Buckminster 'Bucky' Fuller

Richard Buckminster 'Bucky' Fuller was born in 1895 in Milton, Massachusetts. He was a systems theorist (I've no idea what that means, but it might be a euphemism for professional fruitcake), architect, engineer, author, inventor and futurist … which, I suppose, taken all together qualifies him as a bizarre eccentric. As an architect he invented the geodesic dome, and extended the concepts of construction into housing (the Dymaxion House) and transport (the Dymaxion car). He had a few quirks; when travelling he wore three watches, one for the time zone he had left, one for the one he was in, and one for his destination. He proposed the idea of 'Dymaxion Sleep', whereby he could survive with no more than 2 hours' continuous sleep at any time, and invented a new projection for earth maps called the Dymaxion Projection. He also spoke and wrote his own version of (Dymaxion) English, which nobody else could understand.

I wonder how far he took his Dymaxion concepts. Did he, for example, promote the idea of Dymaxion sex? Bucky was a bizarre man indeed, who felt all his Dymaxion inventions would enhance human life. He was therefore an appropriate designer for the Dymaxion car. But how the world survived the demise of all his Dymaxion ideas is a wonder indeed.

The Stout Scarab is included here because it must have taken some skill and nerve to design a car that looked like the offspring of a giant toaster and a juke box, and charge $5,000 for the privilege back in 1936. That 'skill and nerve' belonged to William B. Stout, head of Stout Engineering Laboratories in Dearborn Michigan.

It was probably the first true MPV in the world. It was also technically advanced, with unitary construction, aluminium body, rear engine, 3-speed transaxle, all-round fully independent suspension, and flexible seating arrangements. Only the driver's seat was fixed; the others could be rearranged on the wide floor with the option of sitting around a fold-down table. In spite of looking like a Greyhound bus, it wasn't as big as might be thought; at 16ft it was the same as most medium/large American cars of the day.

But it was unremittingly ugly and cost as much as a Duesenberg, in spite of having basic mechanicals in the shape of a side-valve Ford V8 engine in the back, turning out a paltry 85bhp. Rear view was virtually non-existent so normal parking was next to impossible. Only nine were made between 1934 and 1939, a breathtaking production rate of just under two per year. I suppose it is a reflection of the vast popular appeal of the Scarab that those nine were sold to Stout Engineering Laboratories' directors. Two are known to survive.

Oh, and Scarab is a shortened version of the zoological name *scarabaeus sacer*, which is a species of dung beetle. What an appropriate name for a car that looks like a load of shit.

 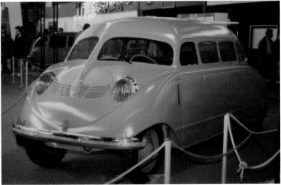

The left side of the brain is supposed to be the coldly logical, verbal and dominant half, whereas the right is imaginative, emotional, spatially aware yet suppressed. I am sure most people (well, maybe just one, and he is my next-door neighbour) have faced that awful dilemma in a morning: do I go to work in the car, get stuck in traffic, raise my blood pressure, risk a stroke, end up being a burden to my family and the state, contribute to global warming etc. (left brain)? Or do I cycle, commune with nature, smell the spring flowers, listen to the dawn chorus, appreciate what life is really about, save the planet, feel high on my natural pheromones, and arrive at work 2 hours late and risk getting sacked (right brain)?

Well, the marketing whizz-kids at Zagato recognised that this fundamental early morning human left/right brain conflict could not always be successfully resolved over a bowl of high-fibre muesli. So in 1992 they designed the perfect vehicle to release us from this torment: the Fiat 500 Z-Eco Zagato. It would keep both sides of our brain happy. This was half a car and half a bicycle rack. You could drive halfway and cycle the rest. The drawback was that you couldn't cycle first and then drive when you were tired, except in the evenings.

OK, as a car it might have had limited appeal. But, with the cycle removed, the little Z-Eco could have made a perfect inner-city environmentally friendly mini-hearse, coffin cosily alongside the passengers, nice for the mourners (or rather, mourner). However, this was a market opportunity apparently overlooked by the guys at Zagato.

It wasn't an ideal car for the young Italian male out on a date, either. I presume his unfortunate lady friend would have to occupy the bicycle seat whilst he was cosseted inside the Zagato. Arriving for the dinner date he would still be smartly dressed, whilst she would be covered in mud and rain and still be picking insects out of her teeth.

Had Zagato taken this basic idea further I suppose we could today have a Rolls-Royce Phantom Zagato Z-Eco complete with chauffeur-peddled tandem, a Range Rover Z-Eco with two mountain bikes, and a Z-Eco Routemaster bus with a rack for seventy bicycles. It's a shame the marketing guys had such a blinkered view of market needs.

Fiat 500 Z-Eco: the answer to a commuter's prayer. (Courtesy of Alvise Seno, Zagato)

Wood-burning stoves are quite fashionable these days, and can look really trendy in a smart, modern warehouse loft conversion or a quaint period cottage. But maybe that is where they should stay. In Germany, following the outbreak of war, the design gurus at Adler thought the wood-burning stove could provide the answer to transport in a fuel-starved country, whilst also creating a homely atmosphere. So came about the Adler Diplomat 3 GS. I am not sure if GS stands for gas stove or not. It was a large six-seater limousine powered by a 6-cylinder engine, in turn fuelled by an ancient Aga cooker burning wood. The wood was carried in sacks on the roof and the gas generator, which turned the wood into charcoal, carbon monoxide and hydrogen, was mounted behind. There were a few technical issues which somewhat limited the car's success:

- The consumption of wood was prodigious, measured in forests per kilometre. Instead of 1kg of petrol it consumed 3kg of wood.
- The driver had to keep stopping to bring down another sack of wood and stoke up the furnace, so it was not ideal for rapid getaways or avoiding enemy attention in battle zones.
- I think today's Health & Safety might not have looked too favourably on a hot wood-burning stove being the first point of impact from behind in the case of a collision.
- It ran out of wood every 50km or less. It was wise not to drive too far away from a forest, and to carry an axe.
- As well as the Aga on the back, there was a complex system of equally heavy filters, settlers, gas cooler, post-cleaner and gas-air

mixer at the front, so in terms of weight distribution it was like a 5-ton dumbbell.

- There was the problem of what to do with the charcoal, which had to be dumped periodically. If attempting to avoid a hostile enemy, a large pile of charcoal beside the road every few kilometres would be a dead giveaway.
- The gas unit weighed around 1,000 tons … OK, a bit less than that, but it did little for the car's handling.
- A full roof of wood made fast cornering slightly on the hairy side.
- Given the all-pervading smell of burning wood, the Diplomat might have proved more popular if it had been fitted with lead-light windows, an inglenook fireplace and a beamed ceiling.
- Another problem was the time it took to get the whole thing working. 'I'm just going out to stoke up the car' must have been a common phrase in Diplomat-owning households.

Wood-burning technology never really took off after the war. I cannot imagine why. Wood burners could have made an interesting class at Le Mans.

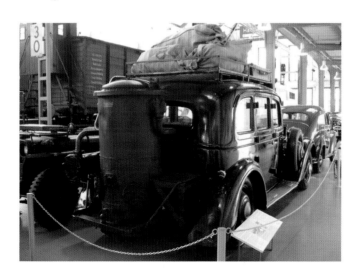

Sir Clive Sinclair is a distinguished inventor and entrepreneur who has brought us the digital watch, pocket calculator and the first practical personal computer back in the 1970s. Even as a teenager he had been dreaming of an electric vehicle, and by the 1970s serious development work was under way at Sinclair Radionics.

Given his experience with personal computers, Sir Clive should have realised that even the most sophisticated processor sometimes needs rebooting in order to continue working properly. Unfortunately, somewhere along the line, Sinclair's

brain clearly experienced a temporary software error, or maybe a bug got past his personal anti-virus protection. When he should have rebooted his brain, he made the mistake of continuing with his revolutionary concept for personal transport. Sir Clive deduced that what the entire world really wanted was a cross between a washing machine, a car battery and a child's pedal tricycle.

OK, the vehicle represented in the photo montage might have required a little bit of development work to get it to market, but that was the essence of the C5: a pedal tricycle aided by a washing machine motor-driven by a car battery.

By the time the C5 was launched, the design and marketing guys had done their bit, and realised the extra spin cycle, and the economy wash and easy care programmes, were of limited use on the road, so the design was slimmed down to the washing machine motor, drive belt, and control system, and the whole lot was concealed inside a plastic shell resembling a sort of enormous white orchid flower.

Technically, it was classified as an electrically assisted tricycle, and it was capable of 12mph (about 11.9mph too much) and sold for £399 (about £398 too much). It wasn't a great commercial success, selling just 12,000 before it was withdrawn in August 1985.

It is difficult to understand why the C5 didn't enter the public's heart. Apart from having dreadful battery life, pathetic hill-climbing ability, no weather protection, just one seat, no gears, almost zero ground clearance, total invisibility from most traffic, no seat adjustment, excessively short cranks for the pedals, a tendency to severely overheat, and a rather weird steering technique involving a set of handlebars below the rider's knees, it was quite a good design really.

It did have one great advantage, though. Being an electrically assisted tricycle, it did not require the 'rider' to have a driving licence, did not require insurance, had no lower age limit, and the driver was not subject to drink-drive laws, as several fortunate individuals found out. On reflection, having seriously inebriated, uninsured, unqualified, 13-year-old 'drivers' tearing around, even at 12mph, in a giant plastic orchid powered by a washing machine motor was not such a good idea after all.

Sinclair promised – maybe threatened is a more appropriate word – to launch a new electric car more in tune with the needs of the market. It was due to appear in 2011.

It hasn't appeared yet. Sir Clive, take your time … and get the 'in tune' bit right this time!

HELICA

The vast majority of cars (well, all cars in practice) are propelled by an engine that turns the wheels, although I did once have an old Ford Escort which had an engine which didn't turn the wheels, just heads, but that's a different story altogether. In 1913 a Frenchman called Marcel Leyat thought it would be an absolutely spiffing idea to dump the boring driven wheel bit and instead strap an enormous propeller to the front of a fragile cycle-car.

The new model Helica.

Now, the observant amongst us might notice a few slightly concerning design features of the Helica. Firstly, the propeller had no shielding so presumably was able to mince up any pedestrians who came too close. It had a single rear wheel which did the steering, so it was the proverbial pig to drive, and the engine was mounted on the roof, so presumably its centre of gravity was so high that even if you had the courage to steer the beast, it would probably topple over on the first bend. Oh, and finally, there were no brakes. But if there had been brakes, given its rather high centre of gravity, it would have toppled forward and turned into a Flymo, useful at times but not in the London rush hour.

Now, I assume le Health et Safety, or whatever they had in France at the time, had a look and demanded some changes. So we then got a new model. In this new incarnation, the propeller was shrouded by a piece of wood about as robust as a damp toilet paper tube, so it would only mince pedestrians immediately in front of it who got sucked in, and the car had a full set of four wheels, but still with the lethal rear-steer, and with the added 'feature' of no Ackermann steering geometry, so it would hop around bends like a demented rabbit.

Amazingly, it is believed thirty were built between 1913 and 1926. Some actually found buyers, and two even survive to this day. However, the original with un-shrouded propeller has long since flown off into the sunset.

I suppose if the idea had caught on today we would have 40-ton Helica Juggernauts sporting twin Rolls-Royce Trent Turbofan engines, racing round the M25 sucking in most of the wildlife, and a fair proportion of the local population, and spewing it all out as mince at the back. Luckily, Messr Leyat's concept faded quietly into the French countryside ... or maybe not quietly, as it made such a din so as to scare even the most robust Gallic spectator.

Range Rover

Most readers will be wondering why on earth the Range Rover is included here as a 'bizarre' car, but there is a very good reason. Wednesday 17 June 1970 is an important date in the history of the motorcar, even though it will not mean much to most. But that was the day the Rover Company announced the iconic Range Rover to the world's motoring press.

This gave birth to the whole luxury 4x4 market, a market in which all major manufacturers now have a foot, or at least a wellie. The idea of an upmarket Land Rover had been mooted back in the early 1950s and the first concept was the Road Rover, which looked remarkably like Postman Pat's van. It was based on the 'Auntie' Rover and had two-wheel drive and little ground clearance. In 1958 a second prototype Road Rover was produced. It combined the looks of a Vauxhall Cresta, a 3-litre Rover, a cheap aluminium greenhouse and a late 1950s hostess trolley.

The Road Rover, resembling Postman Pat's van.

Now we come to the reason why the Range Rover is bizarre. After Land Rover had completed the design of the chassis and all the mechanicals of the final car back in 1970, they told the engineering guys to cobble together some temporary stopgap bodywork so the prototype could be legally road-tested. Apparently, Spencer King, the chief engineer, and senior engineer Gordon Bashford spent about 48 seconds quickly sketching something on the back of an envelope, which then went to the body shop. But when the Board at Land Rover saw it they were in raptures about it, and it was this 'temporary' bodywork which became the iconic Range Rover we know today. It was a car totally designed by the engineers without a whiff from the styling gurus.

Now that's bizarreness at its very best!

The second prototype Road Rover.

The NAMI-013 is included here mainly for one slight technical flaw, which we will come to shortly. Because of this 'flaw' it was redesigned three times between 1949 and 1953, yet remained a single prototype model.

It was actually a six-seater minibus based (loosely) on the Pobeda GAZ M20 we covered earlier. With forward-drive position, a rear-mounted 4-cylinder, 64bhp engine, full independent suspension and automatic transmission, it was quite advanced technically. Unfortunately, as the only one made no longer exists, photos are scarce and their quality is not good. So why is it 'bizarre', apart from the fact that it looks as if it is reversing?

When road-testing started they found out that in addition to its dangerous overheating because the engine was right at the back and the radiator right at the front, an incredible mistake was found in the design of the steering system. Due to an unfortunate oversight, it was necessary to turn the steering wheel in the opposite direction to where you were going. Due to this quite trivial technical problem, the project was stopped.

My suspicion is that, like me, the engineer designing the steering couldn't tell which was the front and which was the back, and put the mechanism in the wrong way round. After that, the design team was either too proud to admit their simple human error, or an excess of vodka made them forget, and development continued. It's a pity in some ways – the 'optional extras' list for the NAMI-013 could have included both 'normal' and 'reverse' steering options.

Any car that can fly must merit inclusion in this book. Many attempts have been made over the years to make flying cars, but one unique feature of the Taylor Aerocar is that it did indeed fly.

The brainchild of Moulton Taylor of Longview, Washington, six were built, starting in 1949. They all featured detachable wings, and a pusher propeller which could be attached to the engine through a port behind the rear number plate. It could apparently be prepared for flight in under 5 minutes.

Each of the six models was similar, being powered by a flat 4 Lycoming aircraft engine developing between 140 and 150bhp. On the ground, as a 'car', it was capable of around 60mph, but once airborne could achieve a maximum of 117mph, with a cruising speed of a leisurely 97mph. They could climb to 12,000ft and had a range of around 300 miles. The 'cars' carried just the pilot and one passenger.

The first Aerocar, N4994P, like the rest of the series, was designed to tow its wings behind it on the road. Of the six completed, one is still flying, and one is stored (in an airworthy condition) and was for sale in 2011 for $1.2 million. The other four are not airworthy, two being in museums and two in private hands, one of which was for sale in 2012 for $2.2 million. Flying cars don't come cheap!

The really bizarre thing about the Aerocar is that it works. Air certification was obtained in 1956 and Taylor reached a deal for serial production with Ling-Temco-Vought providing he found 500 buyers. Unfortunately, he only found 250, so serial production never materialised. Whether flying cars ever could or ever will become more common is not certain. But there must be an appeal for a 500-seat luxury coach which, with wings attached, becomes a jumbo jet. Just think how much easier travelling could be.

The first Aerocar, N4994P.

Gabriel Voisin was what is called in car design circles a 'visionary'. This normally means a total crackpot, who produces cars so weird and way out nobody buys them, and who spends his twilight years naked, squatting on some exotic Far Eastern beach meditating. Generally, of course, this is completely unfair, the biased view of a layman totally devoid of any meaningful understanding of motoring design matters. In Voisin's case, though, it isn't …

All of Voisin's cars were at the unusual end of the scale of exceptional unusualness, but the pinnacle of his 'visionary' creativity came with his Straight 12 model. As the name implies, the engine had 12 cylinders stretched out in a straight line – a very long, straight line. Imagine three normal 4-cylinder engines placed end to end and you have a seriously long engine. Indeed, the engine of this model was so long it protruded into the passenger compartment. The photograph shows the immense bonnet of the Voisin Straight 12.

Well, actually it doesn't. The photo is of a completely different car called a Bucciali, but there is sense in this deception. The Bucciali was originally designed to take Voisin's enormously long engine, hence the huge bonnet. But Mr Bucciali chickened out at the twelfth hour and fitted a V12 instead, at half the length. Photographs of the Voisin Straight 12 seem to be non-existent. There are plenty of photos which claim to be this car, but they generally depict the quite sane V12 instead. It is possible that M. Voisin was so embarrassed by his patently phallic creation that he refused to let any photographs be taken.

Tatra is included here chiefly because this quite amazing and advanced car was kept going for so long, I presume on the basis of the ancient Czech maxim, 'if it ain't broke, no fixski'.

The Tatra company dates back to 1850. In 1897 it produced one of the world's first cars. By the 1930s, under the distinguished Austrian engineer Hans Ledwinka, the company started producing what it became famous for – large, technologically advanced, luxury saloons. These cars were noted for their incredible streamlining and their rear-mounted, air-cooled, alloy V8 engines which make a most distinctive sound.

Production continued during the war as the Germans took a liking to these quirky cars. After the war, the Czech government commissioned Tatra to build new luxury cars for their party 'elite' to replace poor-quality imported Russian cars. In response, Tatra started building the 1930s models again, but with slightly more rounded and enclosed bodies. If the recipe is OK, why change it?

Tatra continued with this same recipe right up until 1999, when

One of the earliest Tatra cars.

the last model, the T700, ceased production. Under that apparently normal front-engined-looking, Italian-designed body is essentially the same rear, air-cooled V8 and chassis first used in the 1930s. Observers will be hard pressed to find any clue that this luxury saloon is air cooled and rear-engined, never mind that it's basically a 60-year-old design! Good work, Ledwinka!

Tatra T700. One of the latest Tatra cars, almost identical underneath.

Czechoslovakia's Secret War Weapon

After Germany invaded Czechoslovakia in 1938, production of the Tatra continued as normal, mainly because the Germans took a liking to the cars. However, the powerful, rear-engined Tatras took some mastering, and many German officers met their death driving the cars too fast around corners with inadequate driving skills. The Tatra thus became known as the Czechs' secret weapon. At one point, official orders were issued from Berlin banning the officers from driving Tatras. I often wonder whether the Allies ever considered mass producing Tatras and leaving them parked around Czechoslovakia with the ignition keys inside for German officers to steal!

Many readers may think it strange to classify the 2CV as 'bizarre'. However, it must be remembered that not all the cars listed here are bad. They are here because, in one way or another, they are simply odd or strange to the degree of being bizarre. The 2CV deserves listing under more than one heading, but I have chosen Bizarreness at the Cutting Edge because at the time it was technologically completely different from anything else that had come before. Given its amazing fifty-one years between prototype and final production, it could equally

be included under the Sell-By Date category.

So why was the 2CV so bizarrely different? All cars are designed to a brief. Most supercars are designed to propel two people at impossible speeds without consideration of price. Limousines are designed to carry a select few in supreme ostentatious luxury. Family cars are designed to carry families. So what was the brief for the 2CV?

Citroen wanted country peasants to graduate from horse and cart to something a little more sophisticated. The brief was for 'an umbrella on

wheels', which would transport a peasant family of four, plus 50kg of farm produce, whether eggs or pigs, to market at 31mph whilst wearing clogs; and it was to be able to cross a muddy ploughed field without cracking any of the farmer's eggs in trays in the back, whilst consuming just two teaspoons of petrol on the return journey.

In some ways it was techno-logically advanced. It had rack and pinion steering, front-wheel drive, and full independent suspension linked front to back like on the later Mini. The twin-cylinder air-cooled engine was designed with about four moving parts, so the whole vehicle was as reliable and robust as a corrugated iron garden shed, which it quite closely resembled. And if damaged, bits of the shed could be unbolted and replaced. It also boasted height adjustable suspension, although this did involve climbing underneath with a pair of spanners to adjust the tie rods. The early versions had a full-length fabric roof which also covered the boot. This was useful if tall loads had to be

A later 2CV.

carried to market, ideal for the rather scarce French giraffe farmers.

The slight downside was that at first it was only equipped with a 375cc engine, delivering a mind-bogglingly small 9bhp. Even though it weighed little more than a cigarette packet, performance was sub-glacial. Its top speed was 40mph, which could be reached in a Porsche-challenging 42 seconds. So slow was the car that, whilst it may be true it would not crack any of the eggs crossing the ploughed field, and would happily carry a pig or two, by the time the vehicle had made it across the ploughed field to the market, the chickens would have hatched and the porkers would have died of old age.

It is also rumoured that when fully laden it could set off in convoy with another 2CV full of the farmer's family, only for the children to grow up, fall in love, get married and have children of their own all before the market was reached. But the 2CV was designed to take such extensions of farmers' families in its bouncy stride.

For a short time it was sold in the US but was not a success. It was said the 2CV driver had to make an

One of the very bizarre 2CV prototypes. Or is it a garden shed?

appointment to join the traffic flow on the freeway, and that the average American family could certainly drive to the diner in the 2CV, but after consuming the typical American fast food meal, they could not fit in for the return journey.

Over its full lifespan of fifty-one years, from prototypes to final model, and the forty-two years of full production, some 3,872,583 2CV cars were made, plus a further 1,246,306 vans. Many variants were made, including a four-door 'limousine' called the Citroneta Azam, a pick-up version, one with

two engines and four-wheel drive like the Twinni Moke, and also a harlequin version mimicking the Polo Harlequin. Later in production a boot was an optional extra to stick on the outside, and this must have been the inspiration for the rear end design of recent large BMW models.

I have personal experience of a 2CV which underlines its bizarreness. I was driving a friend's 2CV when a front tyre blew. There was no effect at all on the handling or steering, just a drop in top speed from 42 to 40mph. I don't think the 2CV really needed tyres at all.

The Car that Runs on Nothing but Air

The Tata/MDI OneCAT is unique. It doesn't run on petrol or diesel. Nor does it run on electricity, cow dung, fermented Cadbury's Creme Eggs, pigeon fart, angel dust or old chip fat. It runs on air, just pure air. So it sort of burps and belches its way along. The photograph shows one working as a taxi. It looks quite normal really. Ugly, but ordinary enough.

It does, however, require quite a lot of air. To obtain this amount of air it has to be stored at a pressure of around 4,500psi (a lot). And even with a large tank to be going on with, the Tata/MDI OneCAT is still limited to an incredible range of 7km, which unfortunately is not sufficient to drive between 'refuelling' stations. So once it has belched and burped its way empty, the MDI OneCAT is presumably left stranded until someone with very strong lungs happens to pass. Even if it reached a refuelling station, it would take about

4 hours to refill the air tank before it could set off on its next 7km. This means it would be extremely difficult for the Indian taxi driver to earn enough money to support a family. But, of course, as he'd be spending 95% of his time 'refilling' his OneCAT, he wouldn't have much time to actually create a family in the first place.

There is also one small technical problem with the OneCAT. When the high-pressure air expands to drive the engine it then cools dramatically, threatening to turn the whole thing into one enormous ice cube. To get around this the air has to be heated by a small burner, which somewhat negates the delightful eco-friendly concept.

The amazing Tucker Torpedo was an unfortunate victim of its own high-tech specification. After the Second World War, the car-buying public was ready for new car designs. However, most of the world's big car manufacturers at first simply rehashed pre-war models, some with designs dating back to the early 1930s. For example, Packard soldiered on with its antediluvian side valve straight 8; in the UK the adventurous William Lyons at Jaguar relaunched the pre-war SS models, although diplomatically replaced the SS name with Jaguar. Even when Jaguar replaced the pre-war model with the Mark V in 1948, this model persevered until 1951, still with the pre-war side valve Standard engine which had first seen service in Lyon's cars back in 1936.

This lethargy by the big manufacturers, caused partly by lack of finance after the war, opened up an opportunity for small manufacturers to fill the 'technology gap'. This is where the Torpedo comes in. In a world full of 'new' side-valve-engined, cart-sprung, reheated pre-war vehicles, the Preston Tucker car was to offer:

- Four-wheel independent suspension by rubber torsion tubes.
- A rear flat 6 water-cooled engine with aluminium block, originally designed for use in helicopters.
- Fuel injection.
- Sophisticated automatic transmission.
- Seat belts.
- A third headlight which turned with the steering.
- A windscreen of shatterproof glass designed to pop out in case of collision.
- An engine and transmission mounted on sub-frames, and complete engine changes possible in 30 minutes.
- A roll bar inside the roof, and a perimeter safety frame.
- A padded safety dashboard.
- A special anti-theft parking brake with separate key.

This specification would not have felt out of place in 1968 never mind 1948. So for 1948 it was a truly bizarre creature. And that was where the problem lay. Just fifty-one Tuckers were made before the company folded up in the wake of negative press coverage, a Securities & Exchange Commission investigation and a heavily publicised fraud trial, all of which was later found to be totally groundless. The rumour is that the 'big three' US car manufacturers, together with 'help' from certain senators, conspired to bring Tucker down.

Incidentally, the name Torpedo was never used officially by Tucker; he preferred the name '48' to avoid any unpleasant wartime memories. Amazingly, nearly all the fifty-one Tuckers made still survive, and when they come up for sale, which is rarely, they go for impressive sums, even up to $3 million.

Amphicar: A Novel Way to Drown

There have been very few successful amphibious vehicles. If 'success' can be defined as simply managing to stay afloat for a while, and having a few eccentric people buy one, then the Amphicar can be classified as a success. But *Time Magazine* included the Amphicar in its list of the fifty worst cars of all time, commenting that it promised to revolutionise drowning, and that it was a lousy car and a lousy boat. Too much depended on the bilge pump keeping pace with the leakage. If it didn't, the Amphicar became an expensive anchor. However, 4,000 were made and 700 still survive, with a rather fanatical following. I don't know how many of the non-surviving 3,300 are parked at the bottom of various harbours and lakes.

It was equipped with the 1,147cc engine from the Triumph Herald, which produced 38bhp. The front wheels provided steering on both land and water, whilst twin screws provided marine propulsion. It was quite heavy at 1,054kg and, as a result, performance was not sparkling. It reached only 7 knots in the water, although 70mph was claimed on dry land, from those brave enough to try. To its credit, it has been described as possibly the fastest car on water and the fastest boat on land – a significant achievement.

In the case of the Rytecraft Scootacar, the photo best highlights how extra-ordinarily similar it was to the ZIS 101 Sport at the beginning of this book.

OK, it looks like a fairground dodgem car with a fake Rolls-Royce radiator. The reason it looks like this is because it *was* a fairground dodgem car with a fake Rolls-Royce grille. Only the large encircling rubber bumpers were removed. It was built by the British Motorboat Manufacturing Company in London between 1934 and 1940. Originally it retained the electric motor of the dodgem, but later a 98cc Villiers engine was fitted. It had a single speed and only one pedal. The clutch was automatic and the single pedal was the accelerator when pushed down, and the brake when released. Also, there was no suspension whatsoever. It could reach a staggering 15mph, which doesn't sound much, but in essentially a kid's pedal car with no suspension, even 15mph must have been pretty hair-raising. And, amongst traffic, it must have been scary to say the least, as highlighted in the lower image. By the time this version was made, the fake Rolls-Royce radiator grille had given way to Rytecraft's own design.

Later cars had two seats, a larger 250cc engine, and normal pedal control. There was even, believe it or not, a commercial version, the Scootatruck. I bet Eddie Stobart wishes he could have a fleet of these for more 'local' deliveries, although it would struggle to deliver more than two packets of biscuits at a time.

Somehow the road-going dodgem with the fake RR grille found its way into the hearts of the British public, and an amazing 1,000 were sold. In the 1960s one intrepid owner drove his 15,000 miles around the world. Several survive and one is on exhibition at the Brooklands Museum.

A Road Legal Dodgem Car

A Car Styled on Tupperware Boxes

The story goes that the wife of one of the directors of the Hunslet Engine Works wanted a car that was easier to park than her Jaguar. The Leeds-based Rodley Automobile Company was set up in 1954, and Henry Brown designed the new car. It was powered by a 750cc twin-cylinder motorcycle engine, and was claimed to be capable of 55mph and 55mpg.

I suspect Brown succeeded in the original objective. It was certainly easier to park than a Jaguar, in a purely physical sense. However, the deep psychological damage of being seen in something styled on a pair of Tupperware boxes and four dustbin lids must have been hard to take. It was a bizarre 'car' to offer a lady used to driving a Jaguar. Maybe Henry Brown was 'on something' at the time. Or maybe the director of the Hunslet Engine Works just hated his wife. Certainly his wife's response to her 'new car' is not recorded, and if it had been, it would probably be unprintable here.

The Rodley Company had ambitious plans to produce fifty cars a week. Over the two years it was in production, they didn't quite manage that. In fact, only sixty-five were made in total, about one per fortnight – or 1% of the target. Why did the British public not take the Rodley to its heart? Here are some possible reasons:

- It was pig ugly and made Tupperware boxes look rather stylish and sporty.
- It was advertised as a four-seater, but there weren't enough families of midgets to keep the business going.
- Steering was by means of chains, so it was as easy and precise to steer as an oil tanker.
- It had a rather disarming habit of overheating, to the extent that it could burst into flames. Maybe a good thing if it took these monstrosities off the road.

It is rumoured that one of the sixty-five built still survives, which fortunately means 98.5% don't. I was unable to track down the sole survivor. This is understandable since, if you owned a Rodley, would you let other people know? The photograph, therefore, is one of the original 'marketing' pictures, and in black and white.

Symptomatic of its extreme bizarreness is the fact that the only other picture I could find of a Rodley, after hours of research, was in the 1955 *Observer's Book of Cars*. The amazing lack of images suggests that not only were people too embarrassed to be seen in one, but they were too embarrassed to be seen photographing one.

If the Rodley were still around today, and still providing viable 'easier parking' options to Jaguar XJs and XFs, I do wonder what it might look like. Even Tupperware has come a long way since 1954. Oh, and a final word. The Rodley was designed by the same guy responsible for the Rytecraft Scootacar. If nothing else, it shows he managed to preserve his sense of humour through the Second World War.

The Atom: The Most Basic Unit of Road Transport

In some ways, the Fairthorpe Atom and the Rodley were competitors. Not, I should point out, competitors for customers, as both had almost no customers at all. Rather, they competed head to head to be amongst the most stupid and ugliest wheeled creations of all time. There are some differences though:

1. The Atom's snot-like appearance makes the Rodley look almost as desirable as an Aston Martin Vanquish. It is indeed fortunate for mankind that only forty-four were made.

2. The Atom made the Rodley look like a supercar; the Atom simply had a 1-cylinder engine of 248cc, and in spite of its appearance, the aerodynamics of a septic tank.

3. In the only road test I could find, no acceleration figures were given as it could not even reach 40mph, which was their first recording speed. Maybe the road tester was not brave enough to try. Neither did the road test include a photograph. I assume it was well into darkness before the testers gave up seeing if it would ever reach 40mph, and the photographer had left for the pub.

4. I understand that no Atoms survive, so by comparison the Rodley, which has one survivor, has some degree of longevity.

The Atom as it was originally designed, complete with Air Vice-Marshal Donald Bennett, the company founder, somewhat sheepishly attempting to escape before the camera shutter went.

The original Atom had 'styling', to use the word loosely, which was definitely bizarre, with a huge bulbous nose, tiny headlamps mounted on top of the wings, and crude side windows giving it the appearance of a truly repulsive carnival mask and a bull frog. On reflection, the name Atom is highly appropriate for this vehicle. The atom is the most basic particle there is which can exist on its own. The Atom has to be the most basic car which can exist on its own.

One serious drawback to the Atom was that there was no provision to cool the engine, so after a long run the car could spontaneously burst into flames. Whilst for humanity's sake that might be a desirable state of affairs, it is unlikely any sane person could drive the Atom far enough for it to get that hot. This was one 'feature' it shared with the Rodley.

Air Vice-Marshal Donald Bennett had been one of the most distinguished RAF chiefs in the Second World War. It's a pity his Atom didn't fly a little better. The atom, as nuclear scientists know, is hard to break. By contrast, the Atom proved only too easy to break, and none survive. For this reason the photographs are of dubious quality … as indeed was the Atom.

The Atom did, however, win at least one great national accolade, which is something in its favour. It was voted, by the website autoshite.com, as the worst car of all time. So it wasn't always a loser.

An 'improved' version of the Atom, called the Mark II; maybe Wart II would have been more appropriate.

Fairthorpe's Other Offerings

In addition to the basic saloon, there was also a drophead Atom, and even a van version, which had four wheels, unlike the basic Atom's three. Given the snail-like performance of the Atom 'saloon', I suspect progress in the van must have been desperate in the extreme; not for delivering perishable goods, for sure.

The Atom developed through three series, growing in engine size up to 650cc. The Atom was never cheap, but by the final 650cc version the price had escalated to over £500. This was a bit of a joke by 1957, just two years before the Mini was launched as a proper car for £497.

OK, the Atom, in all its incarnations, was absolute crap and dire to look at. It was like a wax model of a proper-looking car had been left in the sun a little too long and had started to melt. But Fairthorpe did go on to produce some exciting cars, including one super-lightweight sports car, the Zeta, with a 2.6-litre Ford Zephyr engine, which in its day was one of the fastest cars on the road. With six carburettors, and a cylinder head from BRM, it was certainly a performer. However, in order to keep up the tradition, it was pig ugly and about as robust as a cream doughnut.

Imagine you are back in 1957 – what sort of new car might you market in New York, a city full of Cadillac Eldoraldos, Pontiac Bonnevilles, Ford Thunderbirds and Lincoln Continentals, and where the car buyers are rich bankers, doctors and lawyers? Would you launch:

a A 20ft-long, four-door, six-seat, 7-litre, V8-engined, tail-finned luxury mega-barge equipped with power everything, from steering to toenail clippers?

b A single-seater with zero doors, a single-cylinder 150cc engine, with handlebar steering, a body made from a motorcycle sidecar, turned back-to-front, split down the middle and widened, and then finished off to resemble blue snot?

Any normal person would choose the former. Carl Jurisch, a 'talented' German engineer who had built his own car from scratch aged 24, was clearly not normal, and thought the latter would be perfect for the young Wall Street high-flyer as he whizzed around town. For some reason, which totally escapes me, it was not a success and just three were built, two in blue and one in red.

What was wrong with the concept? It might have had something to do with the fact that Jurisch lived in rural Germany and had never been to the US. His entire knowledge of the States probably came from his school atlas. If you cover the wheels in the photo you'll see the motorcycle sidecar on which it was based.

It is reported that Jurisch brought the car to the office of a German motoring magazine for it to be tested, but was turned away because the magazine staff thought nobody would ever be crazy enough to buy such a thing. The magazine was right. Nobody was.

One of just three Jurisch Motoplans. It really is based on a motorcycle sidecar. (Courtesy of Bruce Weiner, Microcar Museum)

I remember from my childhood the Noddy and Big Ears books, and in particular the car these two drove around in. I always assumed such vehicles only existed in kids' books. But no, I was wrong. Noddy's car does exist, and it is called the Rovin D-2. Noddy's car was, however, better looking and probably had better performance, and a little more room for Big Ears.

The Rovin was the brainchild (I use that word cautiously, 'brain orphan' might be more appropriate) of Robert and Raoul de Rovin. Having built motorcycles and small cars in the 1920s and 1930s, they went on to present at the 1946 Paris Salon the single-headlamp Rovin 'D'. Deciding it probably looked a little too sensible and not sufficiently cartoon-like, they reworked it as the 'D-2'. I assume the 2 meant 'two headlamps' and the D meant 'daft'!

It was fairly successful for a road-going Noddy car, and some 200 were made. With a 10bhp twin-cylinder engine of 425cc, it had a fair performance and could reach 45mph, which would have helped the driver escape from anybody who might recognise him. It was also quite advanced, with rack and pinion steering. The main problem facing owners was where to buy the pointed red cap, and where to find a friend with exceptionally large ears – or indeed any friend at all if they'd actually bought one.

Rovin D-2. One careful owner, Noddy. (Courtesy of Bruce Weiner, Microcar Museum)

The background of the David on its own is enough to rate the car as bizarre. The idea came from Jose Maria Armangue, a bobsled fanatic. There was, however, just one tiny detail which tended to thwart his bobsleighing ambitions: he lived in Spain, which is rather on the warm side. And he lived in one of the warmer parts of Spain, which is also remarkably flat.

Having grown tired of searching in vain for icy, downhill runs to practise his bobsleighing on, he decided to fit wheels to his sled for coming downhill and a small motor to help him get back up again, even though there weren't, in fact, any hills on the hot plains. And so was born the first David microcar.

The business of David S.A. flourished, building taxis, workshops and garages as well as microcars. The microcar which emerged after the war in 1957 was a success, and is the one shown. The engine was integral with the front-driven wheel, and turned with the front wheel when steering, and it was all suspended on a huge, three-quarter elliptic spring. Steering was by a vast white steering wheel working on an enormous pinion, a little like steering a super-tanker in some ways. It also looked uncannily like a large clog.

With a 1-cylinder, two-stroke engine of 345cc, and generating 10bhp, it didn't set the world alight as a car, but as a bobsled it was quite rapid. It could probably knock the spots off any real bobsled, in the hot plains of Spain at least.

Owners of a David did face one unique problem. It was a small car, and if you were a tall driver you'd have to be very careful about where you were heard to say, 'It's a tight fit inside my David …'

The Road Legal Bobsled

The fastest bobsled in Spain. (Courtesy of Bruce Weiner, Microcar Museum)

The Peel P50 holds the title for the smallest car ever to go into production. That alone merits it for inclusion here.

I have a theory that it was going to be a normal-looking, full-size car, and that it was to be designed by three people: one would do the front, one the rear, and a third the bit in between. But on the critical day the first two took a 'sickie' and only the bit in between ever left the drawing board. So what we have is a three-wheeled 'bit in between'. Fortunately, the engine somehow made it into this middle bit, so it was truly mid-engine like all good Ferraris and Lamborghinis. The man who did the

middle bit also managed to find three tiny wheels to make the whole thing mobile, presumably whilst waiting for the front and back to arrive … which they never did.

It was made between 1962 and 1965 on the Isle of Man by the Peel Engineering Company. Fifty were made and twenty-seven survive, which is an above average survival rate for bizarre cars. It had one of everything: one seat, one door, one windscreen wiper, one cylinder, one rear wheel, and one reverse gear … oh no, that's an exaggeration, it had no reverse gear at all. If you wished to do a tight turn, you got out, lifted the rear end, and turned it round manually. After all, it only weighed 59kg, not much more than a bag of water softener salt.

Just 50in long, 39in wide and 47in high, it was almost a perfect cube. With its 49cc DKW engine it could, in the hands of someone sufficiently brave, reach 38mph, and return over 100mpg, although it would have required someone with a strong constitution, a strong bladder, and an IQ to match the engine capacity, to check the 100 miles was actually achievable. What a shame they didn't do a stretch-limo version (a double cube?). I'm sure that in the US we'd have seen a 25ft-long Peel P50 with a supercharged 7-litre V8. To its credit, however, the Peel featured on an episode of *Top Gear* in which Jeremy Clarkson, no midget at 6ft 5in, drove a Peel into the Television Centre and into a meeting via the lift.

Another possibility for the Peel might have been to paint large dots on each of its six almost identical faces and invent a unique form of motoring dice. This could, if carefully planned, also have revolutionised the emergency services' response to accidents. When (rather than if) the unfortunate Peel driver crashed or rolled his car, the emergency services could be alerted to the likely extent of injury and damage from his 'score'. A low 1 or 2 meaning just a front or rear impact, a 3 or 4 a more serious roll on to one side, and a 5 or 6 a full rollover on to the roof.

An attempt has been made recently to reintroduce the Peel as an electric vehicle. Maybe clockwork might be more appropriate. Finally, I have noticed a remarkable similarity between the Peel and some cable car pods – maybe that is where the other twenty-three ended up.

Readers are probably wondering two things: first, what is a BMW doing in the Bizarreness on a Small Scale section of this book? Surely BMW is, and always has been, a manufacturer of large, sporty, luxury saloons, and exciting sports cars? Second, why is there a photograph of a humble Austin 7?

The answer to the first question is yes … and no. The answer to the second question is that yes, it is an Austin 7, but at the same time it isn't an Austin 7. Confused?

The first car BMW made in 1927 was the Austin 7, produced under licence. The car was given the delightful name of Dixi. Whether you like BMWs or not, you have to admit two things: their cars today are high-quality, high-performance vehicles; but they don't produce any car you could call 'cute'. Yet without doubt the little Dixi is an extremely cute car. Whether that merits the title 'bizarre' I am not quite sure, but I couldn't resist including it.

Eventually, in 1932, BMW designed their own car for the first time, the BMW 3/20PS. Was it a massive leap forward in technology? Was it a 150mph world beater or a luxury six-seat limo? No. It was virtually the same as the Dixi, and still used the Austin 7's 788cc engine and front suspension … and chassis, and brakes, and, well, almost everything except the rear suspension, as it turned out. It soldiered on until 1934.

Had the war not completely shaken up all German car production, I cannot imagine what BMW might be turning out today. Maybe they'd still be producing little British cars like the Mini – oh, now I come to think of it, that's exactly what they are doing.

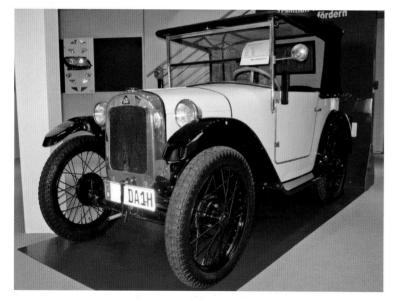

Plain Bonkers

When a company wishes to design a new model, they have a number of options for the bodywork: they can use their in-house design team; they can contract out the work to another manufacturer or a professional design company; or, best of all, they can commission one of the leading Italian design studios, such as Farina, Michelotti, Frua and so on.

The Ardex Company, however, adopted a different strategy. Ardex was set up by Marcel Tamine in Nanterre, Paris. At first they built cycle cars along the lines of the Morgan three-wheeler. But by 1953 they decided the time had come to build a 'proper' car, a four-wheeler. When it came to designing the bodywork, it appears that Marcel decided to save some money and farm out the design to the origami class at the local primary school.

The specification of the Ardex puts a whole new meaning on the word 'basic'. A single-cylinder, 50cc S.A.B.B. motor provided the 'go' (a word used cautiously here), the body was made of plywood and sheets of vinyl, and it was all supported on four bicycle wheels. I assume it only had one headlight because the engine wasn't powerful enough to run two. Surely this makes the BMW M5 look distinctly agricultural.

It was produced for two years, until 1955, and presumably some people actually bought one. However, very few were made in that time. It is interesting to reflect that the previous model to this one, produced under severe austerity measures when petrol engines were as scarce as hens' teeth, had actually been an adult pedal car. As a pedal car the Ardex starts to look a little less bizarre. It might also, of course, have been faster.

A paper car? Maybe it's disposable. (Courtesy of Bruce Weiner, Microcar Museum)

The Car Designed by a Pre-School Origami Class

ZUNDAPP JANUS

After the Second World War, the long-established firm of Zundapp in Nuremberg began to realise that the public wanted a more refined and weatherproof vehicle than the motorcycles and motor-assisted bicycles they were currently offering. Recognising that they could not afford to develop a model from scratch, they hunted around and settled on Dornier's front/rear-facing prototype for development. It was called Janus, after the Roman god who faced both ways, and it faced two fundamental problems:

1   It was truly symmetrical, so it was impossible to tell which way it would drive off. A slight safety issue …

2   The rear passengers faced backwards, a novelty which very quickly faded on the German motorways, where they might see a 3-ton Mercedes 300 Limousine approaching in the same lane, flashing its lights in warning, at up to 250km/h.

I suspect the appearance has a simple explanation. The company could only afford to pay the designer for half the job, so they simply photocopied the front, reversed it, and called it the back. The weight of its robust construction and much glass placed a heavy burden on the 250cc Bella scooter motor, so to say performance was snail-like is an insult to those crustacea. With the 14bhp motor it struggled to reach 48mph.

The plan had been to make 15,000 per year, but in the first six months just 1,731 were made. It was never known if the annual production rate could be reached as production stopped before a year had passed.

The Zundapp Janus. A two-faced car? (Courtesy of Bruce Weiner, Microcar Museum)

Car or Greenhouse?

Provided you have a strong constitution and are sitting down, I will present you with the 1955 Grataloup. I think the problem is clear. The designer started one morning on his design, working from the front backwards. At lunchtime, as it was a nice sunny day, he went to the pub, had a few too many, and when he returned in the afternoon to complete the design he forgot he was designing a car and thought he was designing a small greenhouse. So we got the Grataloup. It looks like a two-seater, but in fact the 'passenger' seat is where the engine is located. It was clearly designed for drivers more into stamp collecting, train spotting or roundabout appreciation than having friends.

Fortunately, the total production run was less than two. And the whole production run still exists, giving a remarkably high survival rate. But the car was a confusing assembly of bits: a 247cc Villiers engine from a BSA motorcycle; a separate gearbox from a French Rene Gillet motorbike; a starter motor connected by a leather belt; suspension by leaf springs, longitudinal at the rear and transverse at the front; steering by a direct link to the steering arms; glazing from the local garden centre and so on. In many ways it resembles a collection of bits from a car boot sale thrown together after a heavy lunch by a demented French mechanic. With a jaw-dropping 7bhp it was claimed to be capable of 53mph, which is slow for a car but quite fast for a small greenhouse.

Somewhere for your tomatoes. (Courtesy of Bruce Weiner, Microcar Museum)

So the designer of the Grataloup went to the pub, got pissed, and returned to the office thinking he was designing a greenhouse. But that was one better than the designer of the Norsjö Shopper. It looks as though he started designing the front, went away for lunch and never returned. It is a little reminiscent of a covered car park ticket machine on wheels.

It was built in Forshaga, Sweden, in the late 1960s and 1970s. When the designer failed to return from the pub, some bright spark thought he could finish the rear using the dumped supermarket trolley he had found that morning. It was staggeringly low powered, with a single-cylinder, 47cc Fichtel & Sachs moped engine and moped-type controls, had handlebars rather than a steering wheel and cable-operated brakes all round. For ease of entry for the single passenger, or 'shopper', the canopy tilted sideways, complete with the handlebars and all the controls. I'm surprised it didn't simply topple over on to its side. In its day it was quite popular and commercially successful, but only one is thought to survive.

The manufacturer claimed it could achieve 60km/h. And it did have a few 'luxury' features. It came in one colour – just one – and it had a padded seat (probably a spare from a Soviet army truck) and a headlight. The vehicle might be explained by two important features of Sweden. Firstly, for half the year the sun doesn't rise, so the country and its car designers are swamped in Stygian gloom. Secondly, to alleviate the depressing impact of month-long nights, alcohol consumption is high. In this context of inebriated total darkness, the Shopper starts to look quite sensible.

The term 'Adult Sports Car' conjures up images of automotive orgies, petrol-fuelled orgasms, naked nymphets writhing over well-oiled bonnets, and quite unmentionable things being done with dipsticks. Unfortunately, in the case of the Eshelman Adult Sports Car nothing could be further from the truth.

Cheston L. Eshelman deserves a prize for redefining the word 'basic' when applied to the motorcar. Eshelman manufactured garden tractors and rotary tillers. This experience with agricultural machinery made him perfectly qualified to manufacture a 'car', which was a cross between a wheelbarrow and a sit-on mower. In fact, his enthusiasm ran away with him, and in 1956 he made a range of four motorised wheelbarrows, sorry, cars: the Sports Car, the Child's Sports Car, the Adult Sports Car, and the Model 200.

These 'cars' were notable for a number of reasons: there was no suspension; no charging system for the battery (which had to be removed); the brakes were wooden paddles rubbing on the tyres; drive was to one wheel then by belts to the others; starting was by pulling on a rope; and the engine could only be stopped by reaching into it through a small hole and pressing the 'kill' button. It was also extremely heavy for its size, owing to the extensive use of cast parts.

The Adult Sports Car was powered by a 2.25bhp Briggs & Stratton petrol engine more normally found in small lawnmowers. It could achieve 30mph, quite fast for a wheelbarrow, and return 70mpg. For the more power-crazy customer Eshelman offered a deluxe version, with an eye-watering 2.75bhp. Oh, and it was available in a wide range of colours; that is, yellow.

Redefining the Meaning of 'Basic'

The 'deluxe' version of the Eshelman Adult Sports Car, distinguished from the base model by a thin cushion seat and a chrome-plated plastic 'rocket' on each side. (Courtesy of Bruce Weiner, Microcar Museum)

If the old lady who lived in a shoe had ever developed an urge to get a set of wheels, she wouldn't have had to look much further than the Corbin Sparrow ... now apparently renamed the much less delightful Myers Motors MmG. If Mr Corbin or Mr Myers had asked the team to design a car which could be mistaken for a shoe, he could hardly have been more delighted.

The shoe came in two models, known, bizarrely, as 'Pizza But' and 'Jelly Bean'. Having only one seat, the old lady couldn't have transported any of her children, but since she had so many, the family allowance would have come in handy to buy several Sparrows, one for each offspring.

The Sparrow was electric driven, powered by a 20kW motor with a range of 20–40 miles and a rather frightening top speed of 70mph, making it the fastest shoe in the world. Thirteen 12-volt batteries in series delivered a voltage of 156 volts to the motor, which could peak at 40bhp, or run continuously at 25bhp. The batteries made the Sparrow no lightweight at 1,350lb. Rapid shoes don't come cheap, however; the Jelly Bean had a pre-tax list price of around $30,000. The company recently went out of business, so the shoe is no longer made.

The electric shoe could achieve the equivalent of around 162mpg, which slightly makes up for the outrageous price and the fact that it makes you look a complete prick. Although not for the straight-laced, it is definitely a car with sole ... but you had to be fairly well heeled to buy one! (Ed., that's enough, it's pathetic!)

The Briggs Stratton Flyer is bizarre on a number of grounds. Just its name conjures up images of lawnmowers, and with good reason. The engine developed for the Flyer was the parent of generations of lawnmower motors.

So, why was the Flyer 'bizarre'? Let's look at the facts:

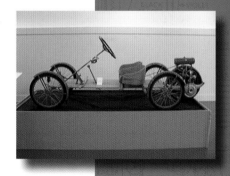

- It had no bodywork whatsoever.

- It had no suspension whatsoever. The flexible wooden 'chassis' was the only suspension, and as a result there was no damping at all.

- With a lawnmower engine, and made from a few planks of wood and little else, it is probably the only car ever built which could be assembled from items bought in the local B&Q.

- The engine wasn't actually part of the car itself, but was attached to a fifth wheel which hung over the rear.

- There were no gears and no clutch. The engine was started with the fifth wheel raised, and then this was gently lowered on to the road to move off.

- It had one of the lowest power outputs of any car ever, at just 2bhp in the later models. Earlier models had even less power. Mind you, its weight was similar to that of a packet of crisps, so progress was better than expected.

- It was available in a wild variety of colours, as long as you chose red.

- According to the *Guinness Book of Records*, the Flyer was the cheapest car of all time, costing between $125 and $150 depending on 'specification' (however, the options are not recorded).

Incredibly, the Flyer sold quite well and a number still survive. It also spawned a magazine called *Motor Wheel Age*, which was solely concerned with 'fifth wheel' propulsion. It is still possible to buy blueprints for the Flyer for anyone interested in building one – anyone with a B&Q nearby.

The Car You Could Build in B&Q

I've often noticed that it seems to take more words to say something in French than it does in English. Maybe that's why they take longer lunch breaks. All conversations take longer. For example, on aeroplanes the English notice about your lifejacket simply says 'lifejacket under seat'. Alongside this the French notice may be loosely translated as 'your vest of life safety is located underneath your seat' – ten words instead of three.

And the same is true of cars. We have the Mini; the French have La Voiture Electronique Porquerolles. I think it means something like 'why in ****'s name have a car electronique which makes you look un prat complete?'

In 1969 this vehicle was introduced as 'a revolutionary new

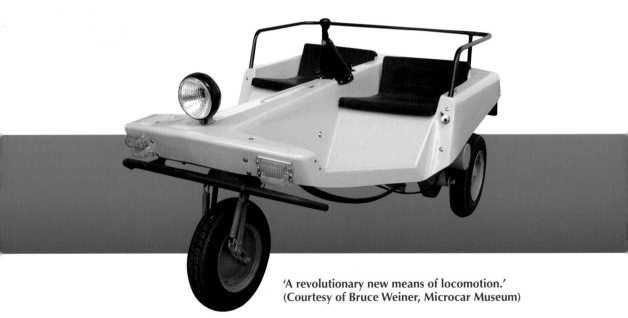

'A revolutionary new means of locomotion.'
(Courtesy of Bruce Weiner, Microcar Museum)

means of locomotion adapted for the constraints of today's lifestyle, for short hauls of 50m to 50km by one or two people'. I have to say that, personally, I don't feel like my life is constrained in such a way that I need to drive around in a motorised wheelbarrow for 50m, never mind 50km. The vehicle was unusual in that it only had one control, a single central joystick to perform the functions of acceleration, braking and steering. The front wheel was just a freely moving castor, steering being achieved by speeding up the electric motor of one wheel relative to the other. Accidently touch that stick with your knee when 'boarding' and there is no way to predict what might happen. It claimed to be an 'electronic' rather than an electric car. My PC is also electronic – I think I'll stick to that for the time being, even though it will not take me to the supermarket.

The single control was called the 'Stil' after the classical Greek column: a symbol of purity, simplicity and elegance. If elegance means imitating a bag of garden compost in a wheelbarrow, simplicity means the vehicle is devoid of almost everything, and purity is something to do with looking a total prat in public, then the name given to the stick is quite appropriate. I rather think that 'stick' is what you'd receive a lot of if you were seen driving it.

Perhaps the most bizarre feature of the Lavatory Electrical Porcupine, or whatever it's called, is that they managed to sell 200 of them! Perhaps most buyers thought they really were wheelbarrows and used them as such, and in that role they may have been first rate. And, encouraged by this success, they went on to produce two more models, the CAB (which had a roof of sorts) and the COB (with full body).

On all models, however, I think the second seat might have been redundant. Would anyone who owned one of these have any friends? Or maybe the spare seat was for your psychiatrist.

The Velorex Oskar hails from what used to be Czechoslovakia, and was produced between 1953 and 1971. It was built by two brothers, Mojmír and František Stránský, who were said to have been inspired by Morgans. I do wonder if they had ever actually seen a Morgan. OK, there were some similarities: both had three wheels, and, well … that's it. Apparently *oskar* means 'cart on axle', and *velorex* is a combination of 'velo' for bike and 'ex' for export, as they planned to export most of them, assuming they could find enough gullible foreign buyers to take them. But to be fair, the Oskar was a commercial success.

At first sight the vehicle looks like the product of an illicit liaison between a First World War flying helmet and an army tent. I can also pick up clear design DNA from the standard issue Second World War gas mask. It was powered by a rear-mounted, air-cooled, two-stroke motorcycle engine of 125cc or 250cc. It had a hand-operated 'kick' starter and as the engine could be reversed, it had four forward and four reverse

gears. As a result, rather frighteningly, it could go as fast in reverse as forwards, albeit with virtually zero visibility through the tiny rear window. Costs were kept low by using vinyl fabric stretched over a welded steel cage, attached by 'turn-button' fasteners. Get confused over fasteners when getting in and I presume the whole thing could disintegrate into a pile of fabric and bones.

For an oversized motorised flying helmet it had an amazingly successful career, over 15,000 being produced over an eighteen-year lifespan,

including as invalid vehicles. In 1996, 63% of the Oskars made still survived, and many are around today and have a cult following, possibly amongst not only microcar enthusiasts but also vinyl fetishists.

In 1959 the company added a new model, with four wheels and a 350cc engine. Nevertheless, this is said to have suffered seriously from competition from 'vastly superior' vehicles. The fact that these 'vastly superior' vehicles were actually Trabants puts the Oskar's qualities in some perspective.

A car which can be folded up and stored in a suitcase must be some sort of dream. Scrap all multi-storey car parks and simply replace them with large left-luggage facilities. No need for a garage at home, just a small cupboard.

Well, it wasn't just a dream for Engelbert Zaschka who, in Berlin in 1929, designed a foldable car. It wasn't a success. I suspect the ordinary car-buying public might have worried about the car deciding to spontaneously fold up when doing a steady 30mph, the vehicle's breathtaking top speed.

Unfortunately, the surviving photographs of the car are of very poor quality … which seems appropriate as the car was total crap, albeit neatly folding crap. Had Zaschka taken his ideas forward, I have no doubt that folding tanks could have given Germany the upper hand in a number of theatres of war after 1939.

The Mitsuoka Viewt could qualify as bizarre just on the basis of its bonkers name. But it has a much more important reason for being here. If you've ever wondered what the offspring of a Mark 2 Jaguar and a Nissan Micra would look like, well wonder no more. It is the Mitsuoka Viewt.

This basically *is* a Nissan Micra remodelled to look like a bonsai version of Jaguar's iconic sports saloon. To me that's seriously bonkers, on a par with clothing a Sinclair C5 in a replica E-type body or putting a Ferrari F40 body on a Transit van. First introduced in 1993, it didn't quite match the Jaguar's XK engine in the power stakes. Its 1.0- or 1.3-litre Nissan Micra engines (later enlarged to outrageous 1.2, 1.4 and 1.5 litres) were matched to either manual or automatic transmission. It was also offered as a convertible, which is, of course, one up on the Jaguar, which never had this option.

Whilst many people might think the Viewt cute, it is potentially very dangerous on the road. Its front looks so much like the Mark 2 Jaguar that, if seen in the rear-view mirror, any normal driver would assume the 'Jaguar' was at least twice as far away

as its miniature clone actually was, with potentially fatal results.

The Viewt gave Mitsuoka a huge publicity boost, and this allowed them to become recognised as a 'proper' car manufacturer in Japan (although I do wonder how the word 'proper' translates into Japanese). It also spurned rival Japanese car makers to revive the looks of other classic cars, such as the Vanden Plas Princess 1100, and to introduce a whole genre of retro-styled cars. For some reason, however, even the Japanese never got the urge/nerve to revive the looks of the Austin Allegro or Morris Marina.

Mitsuoka: A Bizarre Car Company

Mitsuoka is indeed a very bizarre car company. Founded in 1968 in Toyama City, Japan, it has specialised in making modern-day replicas of classic British cars from the 1950s and 1960s. It is only a small company, with 580 employees, and its replicas are not like normal replicas. They are usually much smaller and all have a sort of caricature element to them, making them the sort of vehicle you'd expect to see in a children's book.

In addition to the Viewt, they make or have made:

Himiko	A replica Jaguar XK150 based on a Mazda MX5.
Galue	Available as either a fake Rolls-Royce or a fake Bentley.
Yuga	A replica London taxi.
Zero	A fake Lotus Super 7.
BUBA 356	A replica Porsche 356 (OK, not British this time).
Ray	A fake Riley Elf, although why anyone would want a fake Riley Elf completely escapes me.
Cute	This looks like a cross between a Nissan Micra and a Rover 400, with the worst stylistic elements of both.
Like	This is 'like' a cross between a Ford Ka and a toaster, and like a toaster, is electric.

Oh, and they also make a supercar, the Orochi, which is actually quite good looking.

A Car Based on a Wheelie Bin and a Cable Car Gondola

The Honda Caren could have been included under Bizarreness in Very Small Helpings on the grounds that it is very small and bizarre. However, I have no hesitation in declaring it Plain Bonkers. The Caren looks like a cross between a wheelie bin, a telephone kiosk and a cable car gondola, and it appears to be supported on a single wheel. But that is an optical illusion.

The reality is that the Caren is actually a moped and sidecar, covered by a telephone kiosk – sorry, all-enveloping bodywork – with a single seat. It came with an impressive and totally essential range of 'extras': neon lighting around the windscreen; a chrome 'spinner' on the sidecar wheel; a musical multi-tone horn; and a monstrous sound system, so powerful that if you turned the volume to full the car stopped as all its power drained away. The owner could therefore drive around suburban Tokyo not only frightening the public with its mobile phone booth, but also deafening and dazzling them all at the same time. It would be the perfect set of wheels for a non-too successful leprechaun

pimp, or a drug dealer who's never moved beyond flogging paracetamol and ibuprofen.

Fortunately, it was not over-endowed in the power stakes. A 50cc single-cylinder engine wheezed asthmatically to churn out 3.8bhp, which enabled a top speed of 35mph. Any faster and sharp braking might well have resulted in a series of somersaults. I also suspect that when the large door was hinged fully open, as shown, it was likely to topple over, having already killed or maimed any pedestrians standing in front or at the side. Once open, the door must have been quite difficult to close, as the interior handle was then about 10ft away from the seated driver.

The single seat meant no passengers. This couldn't have been a problem as who would want to be a passenger in a Caren anyway? Another slight issue is with the name, of course; the simple statement 'I found it quite difficult to get inside your Caren', if overheard, might possibly be misunderstood.

The Honda Caren: a telephone box on wheels. (Both images courtesy of Bruce Weiner, Microcar Museum)

The Octoauto was conceived by Milton Reeves in 1911. Basically, he took a perfectly normal 1910 Overland and added two more axles and four more wheels. The resulting vehicle was over 20ft long. His logic was that having eight rather than four wheels would halve the tyre wear. The slight flaw in his logic was, of course, that you had twice as many tyres to wear out, so the net benefit was absolutely zero.

It is recorded that Reeves had extremely poor eyesight. One possible explanation for the Octoauto is that Reeves had double vision, so

when he saw his creation with four axles he thought it was just his eyes playing up and in fact it had just two.

Apparently, following its first public showing on the occasion of the first Indianapolis 500, a complete lack of orders for his Octoauto didn't discourage him in any way at all. In 1912 he tried again to interest the motoring public with the Sexauto, which had just three axles. Surprisingly, he didn't get any orders for that either; I would have thought at least some potential buyers would have misunderstood the 'sex' bit of the name and bought one out of

erotic curiosity. I suppose if he had continued long enough he'd have come up with the Quadroauto, a novel concept with two axles and four wheels.

To his credit, Reeves wasn't completely mad, as he is credited with the invention of the exhaust licenser.

Chantecler: the Road-Going Rooster

This car deserves inclusion as bizarre on two grounds. Firstly, it is probably the only car ever made whose name sounds more like a high-class ski resort or a box of liqueur chocolates than a road vehicle. Secondly, it looked like some sort of domestic appliance covered by a tarpaulin. When finished in white it just needed a carrot inserting between its headlamps to make a motorised snowman's head. Its name Chantecler actually meant 'rooster', which fits quite well since its overall appearance was similar to an ostrich egg.

It was, to use the word loosely, 'powered' by a 125cc Ydral two-stroke engine with a rather unusual form of starter, a Westinghouse Gyrostarter. By repeatedly pulling on a lever it wound up a flywheel with a whining sound. When up to full speed the handle was released and a clutch engaged, whereupon the flywheel started the engine. With its massive output of 6bhp it could achieve 75km/h (47mph), for any driver brave enough to try and, of course, not too tired from winding up the Gyrostarter!

Over its short life around 200 were made, but few are thought to survive. Maybe they all 'hatched' and the Loire Valley is now full of Chante-chicks running around. Anyway, the death of the proprietor and inventor in 1957 brought the production to a premature end after just one year. I presume nobody else had the appropriate sense of humour, or nerve, to continue manufacture.

Bizarre Car Names: Part 5

The final selection of car names comes from the Japanese, who seem to have turned it all into an art:

- Nissan Big Thumb
- Mitsubishi Chariot Grandio Super Exceed
- Mazda Bongo
- Mazda Bongo Brawny and Friedee (sub-brands of the Bongo)
- Isuzu Mysterious Utility Wizard
- Isuzu GIGA 20 Light Dump
- Yamaha Pantryboy Supreme
- Honda Life Dunk
- Daihatsu Charade Social Pose
- Daihatsu Naked
- Toyota Deliboy
- Mitsubishi Townbox
- Mitsubishi MUM 500 Shall We Join Us
- Brilliance It's Me (however, this one's from China)

And we finish off with the Hummer: the Hummer was a great success with the gay community and the manufacturer couldn't work out why. Apparently, in certain gay communities 'hummer' is slang for a certain type of gay oral sex. Just be careful where you might be heard to comment, 'I fancy a Hummer'.

Achieving True Bizarreness in the Automotive World

Having reviewed some of the most unusual vehicles of all time, are there some basic rules which must be applied if a car designer wishes to enter the rarified world of the bizarre elite? Based on the findings here, some of the golden rules an aspiring designer might follow are:

- Cars which look like cars are boring. Why make a car car-like when with just a bit of imagination it can look like a wheelbarrow, a dung beetle, a snowball or toadstool? The lesson here is to take the basic design cues from a random search of the dictionary. In just a few moments, with the help of the Concise Oxford Dictionary and a pin, I came up with a number of ideas for a new car: wheelie bin, skin graft, haemorrhoid, coal scuttle ... and so the list can go on.
- Abandon any sense of practicality. People don't *have* to carry luggage; they don't *have* to have friends; they *can* squeeze through impossible apertures to enter the right vehicle. Roofs are for wimps, as are windows, unless they are totally opaque.
- Add some technological 'features' (which, as we know, is the modern manufacturer's term for 'design faults'). Steering which works in the opposite way from expected is a good one, and rear-wheel steering can be a real hoot. The square steering wheel's been done, but think of the other exciting possibilities: triangular, crescent-shaped, romantic heart shape, no steering wheel at all – just a cucumber.
- Certainly don't make the car normal size, by which I mean anything between 6ft long to 25ft long. You'll be simply doing a 'me too' design. Go for small ... can a car be less than 27in long? Or extreme length – the 50–60ft sub-category is currently under-populated and could offer a niche market.
- For heaven's sake don't base the price on cost. Cost plus pricing is for commodities and wimps – price according to desired brand image. Anyone can buy a wheelbarrow for £20; only a select few could afford to buy a motorised one-seat wheelbarrow for £860,000. Exclusivity and image can be created by simple details like price points; a price ticket of £860,000 shows that you yourself value the brand and its attributes. Also, it uses the 'emperor's clothes' strategy: charge £860,000 and everyone will assume it has something so special it's worth every penny, even if it's total crap.
- Eco credentials can help as long as they are not sensible ones. Everyone is doing a 'hybrid', but what about cow dung as a fuel – especially if the car is large enough to carry its own herd of fuel producers?

- Adopt some unique technological details. Think outside the box. What about five or seven wheels rather than the boring, normal four; or two or more engines, especially if one is used for forward and the other for reverse; or how about a 4x3? Everyone has a 4x4 and 4x2, but it would be a corking idea to have four wheels, only three of which are driven. Or even just one ... a 4x3 or 4x1. This could be combined with biased steering specifically aimed at drivers who prefer to turn left rather than right. Such drivers can minimise the delays involved in right turns, just as UPS Parcel vans are routed. That would be what marketing gurus call a 'unique selling proposition'. It would also save tyre wear.

- Invent a new sector. There are plenty of 'sectors' around, like MPV and SUV, and most people have absolutely no idea what the initials stand for. If the manufacturer cannot decide which sector to be in, they call their vehicle a 'crossover'. Given all this complexity, it is so easy to claim your car is the first GDV on the market (without telling the market it actually stands for Gullible Dipstick's Vehicle).

- Finally give the car a totally bonkers name. This is important to establish bizarre credibility. The Japanese are excellent for inspiration here. Often, the bonkers name flows naturally from the brand name, so we could imagine:

Honda Has-wheels
Buick Blok-o-metal
Bentley Bonkers
Chevrolet Can-go
Vauxhall Very
Renault Reasonably-good
Land Rover Lollipop
Chrysler Come Drive with Meeee
Hummer Haemorrhoid Hybrid

So, take all this together and it is easy to think up exciting new automotive concepts. Here's one: a Bentley Bonkers Twin-Eco-Power, named after the legendary Sir Caspar Bonkers, the first blind man to win Le Mans; it is a 56ft-long, seven-wheeled, 15-ton, 25-seat, single-door MPV/SUV/Limousine/Coupe/Pick-up/Fork Lift Crossover, powered by two cow-dung-fuelled engines, one with 17 cylinders and the other 35 cylinders, with a 37-stall cowshed, solar panels and hydroelectric hybrid back-up powered by on-board reservoir, costing £4.5 million or £29.8 million with the optional 'sports' pack (which consists of a couple of cheap plastic side flashes, a special flashing 'sports' gear selector knob, and a deluxe heated cup holder).

Of course, nobody will buy one. But in thirty years' time it could be the main star of another book like this one! And that will have been worth all the effort of a team of highly trained, dedicated and completely mad engineers and designers.

The Most Bizarre Car of All Time is ...

Having finished writing this book, I was faced with a difficult challenge. The publisher wanted me to pick the most bizarre car of all time. What would this turn out to be? Was it:

- A 58ft-long, emerald-encrusted, 8-wheeled Maharajah's limousine styled in the shape of an Indian elephant and running on dried water buffalo dung?
- A single-wheeled gyroscopic, 200-seat, three-deck super bus which can take to the air and also travel under water at 60 knots?

- A disposable inflatable car small enough to carry in your pocket and costing 28p for a pack of six?
- A supercar so hideously fast it gets you to your destination even before you've started to think about where you want to go, returns 20,000mpg and costs less than a pint of beer?
- An edible car made from dry spaghetti, rice paper, digestive biscuits and liquorice allsorts, designed to combat the outrageously high prices of food at motorway service stations?
- An invisible car which allows you to get from A to B without C ever finding out?

Well, no. However appealing they seem, it wasn't any of these. This is in part because of the quite trivial detail that none of these ever existed. But, having thought at length, and in the process having substantially boosted the share price of a number of major distillers and a couple of prime vineyards, there could only be one contender: the VW Polo.

Now before you storm down to Trading Standards to complain under the Trade Descriptions Act or demand back the price of this book, let me explain. Yes, it is the VW Polo. But it's no ordinary Polo. It's the 1994 VW Polo Harlequin, the only car, and possibly the only item ever, to graduate from April Fool's joke to real commercial success.

Every year on 1 April the *Daily Telegraph* runs a spoof advertisement. These have included the left- and right-handed Mars Bar, white Guinness with a black head to promote racial equality, left-handed burgers in Burger King, USB-powered fondue sets for snacking whilst surfing, and dog-repellent paint for BMWs.

On 1 April 1993 VW advertised a Polo aimed at customers who couldn't decide what colour to buy. The Harlequin had each body panel in a different colour. It was, of course, meant as a joke, but the response from the public was overwhelming! VW were inundated with potential customers wanting to buy the Harlequin and in response made an initial 1,000. Then public demand led to 3,800 eventually leaving the factory between 1994 and 1998. According to the DVLA, there are still seventy-four Harlequins on the road in the UK.

One advantage of the Harlequin was that if one of the body panels began to rust, you could replace it in any colour from an old car at the breaker's yard. It was a genius idea. I don't know why the likes of Rolls-Royce, Bentley and Aston Martin have not followed suit!

The Harlequin has to set the gold standard for bizarreness. It is also proof, if needed (yes, I think proof is needed), that the Germans have a sense of humour. However, there is a rumour that VW actually planned the Harlequin as a serious vehicle to address a real consumer need amongst indecisive Germans, and only invented the April Fool's joke when they discovered everyone else in Europe was laughing at them.

A Final Word

It's easy, and maybe not totally fair, to make fun of some car designers. But this book has highlighted just what sort of 'vehicles' these designers have imposed on the world. However, life would be duller without eccentric designers and their creations, so I hope we will continue to see bizarre car designs for many years to come. I've only covered a small part of the 'bizarre' motoring world; there are many more which deserve inclusion but for which space was too limited.

Oh, just as an afterthought. There is one car I have not included as bizarre in spite of its rather bizarre name – the Bizzarrini. In spite of having perhaps the most perfectly bizarre name, the Bizzarrini was anything but bizarre. It was a range of supercars made in Italy by Giotto Bizzarrini, a most distinguished engineer who had worked for Ferrari, Alfa Romeo and ISO. Below is a photograph of the Bizzarrini P538S, powered by a 5.3-litre, Corvette V8 engine, and capable of around Mach 0.9 and 0–60 in 2.3 milliseconds … all right, I exaggerate, but it was mega-fast. I suppose you could call that bizarre, but for all the right reasons.

The Bizarre-ini. (Courtesy of Brett Weinstein)